DATE DUE

JOSTEN'S 30 508

Beginning Badminton

Judy Hashman and C. M. Jones

ARCO PUBLISHING COMPANY, INC.

New York

Note

Published by Arco
Publishing Company,
Inc. 219 Park Avenue
South, New York, N.Y.
10003

Printed in Great Britain

The authors would like to emphasize that although the book has been written for the right-handed player, it applies equally well in reverse to the left-handed beginner. There should be no difference between these players in ability to learn the game.

Library of Congress Cataloging in Publication Data

Hashman, Judy Devlin.
  Beginning badminton.
  1. Badminton (Game) I. Jones, Clarence Medlycott,
1912- joint author.   II. Title.
GV1007.H33 1977   796.34'5   77-5535
ISBN 0-668-04265-6 lib. bdg.

Contents

Introduction

In almost every sport there have been great champions whose success derived primarily from great qualities of character. There are others, probably fewer in number, who have exceptional motor skills. And in a small number of instances there are men and women who have been blessed with both qualities and who have become legendary figures in their particular fields. One thinks of Sir Jack Hobbs and Sir Donald Bradman in cricket, Sir Stanley Mathews in soccer, Jack Nicklaus in golf, Donald Budge and Maureen Connolly in tennis. But in badminton one, and only one, giant figure exists – Judy Hashman. Daughter of a famous player, J. F. Devlin, she inherited his immense motor skills and dedication to the game and has added to them a sense of perfection, uncompromisingly pursued, which enabled her to dominate the world badminton scene for a decade and a half, during which time she won the All-England Championship no less than seventeen times. Her unparalleled knowledge of the game has been reinforced by her qualification as a teacher of badminton and tennis. She further strengthened her experience of working with young people by becoming a school teacher.

Jimmy Jones, former Davis Cup player and Editor of *Tennis* whose experience in coaching Wimbledon stars has won him international recognition, has developed over a number of years methods of training and coaching which have achieved remarkable results at the highest levels. Many of these coaching and training techniques can be used as effectively in badminton as in tennis and that is how this book came to be written.

1 Before you play

Badminton is played with a shuttlecock, or shuttle which is hit back and forth across a net by players using rackets, strung with gut or synthetic fibre.

It is great fun and the fun usually begins immediately because most novices find it comparatively easy to hit the shuttle over the net. Rallies are possible right from the start, even if only from close to the net and using somewhat unorthodox shots. Refinements of stroke play and use of the whole court follow naturally.

You can begin badminton even before you start school and continue it well into old age. As it is an indoor game you will never have to rely on good weather. Boys and girls, men and women can enjoy mixed doubles together, a fascinating combination of skill, subtlety and speed.

Singles, one man against another or one woman against another, men's doubles and ladies' doubles are the other events staged in match, tournament and championship play.

The rackets used weigh little, normally between 5 and $5\frac{1}{2}$ ounces (140 to 155 grams) and are about 26 inches (65 centimetres) long. Even a toddler can manage the weight of a parent's racket, though not always the circumference of the handle.

So the first task is to buy or borrow a racket which can be held easily and manoeuvred swiftly and smoothly, because badminton is a fast game.

The shuttle weighs from 73 to 85 grains (4 to 5 grams) and has fourteen to sixteen feathers on a kid leather skin, fixed into a cork head about one inch (25 millimetres) in diameter. The feathers slow the shuttle down towards the end of its flight, so giving the game its unique character.

Before trying to play, watch good players in action. Study the best players in your club or area. Look for their strengths; study their positioning. Continue to watch better players as you move up the ladder. By all means experiment with strokes and tactics which you see others use. Remember always, however, that you are a unique person who should be seeking to develop your own, individual methods of play.

Badminton is an overhead game in which ninety per cent of shots are struck above shoulder height. Thus, anyone who can throw strongly starts with an important advantage. 'Throw strongly' needs amplification and qualification. The throw must be of the type used by pitchers in American baseball. *Figure 1* shows the action. In *(a)* the left shoulder is pointing at the target and the right forearm is lined up along the line the shuttle is to travel.

In *(b)* the thrower is 'exploding'. His right arm is upright, his body has pivoted so that his shoulders are facing the target and his knees have straightened, so adding extra power to his body thrust. All this has swung the left shoulder backwards and the left arm downwards past the left leg.

In *(c)* the throw has been completed, showing that every scrap of his arm, body and knee strengths have been combined to give maximum power to the throw. This has been supplemented by a strong wrist flick during the moment of releasing the shuttle.

Badminton is played indoors on a court 44 feet (13.2 metres) long by 20 feet (6 metres) wide for doubles and 17 feet (5.1 metres) wide for singles. The court is divided into two halves by a net 5 feet (1.5 metres) high in the centre and 5 feet 1 inch (1.52 metres) high at the posts. The court is marked by lines as shown in diagram 2. When space is limited, a court for singles only can be marked out by eliminating lines X and Y.

The ceiling should never be less than 28 feet (8.5 metres) from the floor. No distances between the back or side lines and the court surrounds are stipulated in the laws of the game, but 3 feet (0.9 metres) is normally considered acceptable.

The lines show the limits of the court, both for service and general play. Any shuttle which is allowed to drop to the ground must miss the line completely to be judged out. Even if the extreme edge of the shuttle just touches the very

Figure 1 The first requirement when starting badminton is the ability to throw a shuttle correctly and strongly.

outside of the line, the shot is judged 'in' and the player (or pair) who let it fall loses the point.

Only the server can actually score points. In singles if server A loses a rally, the score is unchanged but service goes to server B who is now in the position to score points. When, in turn, he loses a rally, service reverts to A, who can resume scoring points.

At first, badminton scoring may seem a little complicated and we want you to try your hand with racket and shuttle, so for the moment simply play until you or your opponent reaches a score of 15. Then start another game.

Rule-book scoring is given in the Appendix.

Before starting, the players toss, usually by spinning the racket. The winner can say:

> '*I'll serve*', in which case the loser of the toss has the right to choose the end of the court from which he will play the first game, *or*
> '*You serve*', in which case the loser can also choose his end, *or*
> '*I'll start from this end*', in which case the loser may decide either to serve or to receive service.

The contestants change ends on completion of the first game and again after the second. If a third game is needed – matches are usually the best of three games – the players change ends mid-way through it (see Appendix A).

Each game begins with a service from right court to right court. If the server wins the point, he then serves from left court to left court, and so on, alternating. As soon as he loses a rally, his opponent serves from right to right. Thereafter each server starts from the right court if an even number or left court if an odd number.

The feet of both the server and the receiver must be inside their respective service courts until after

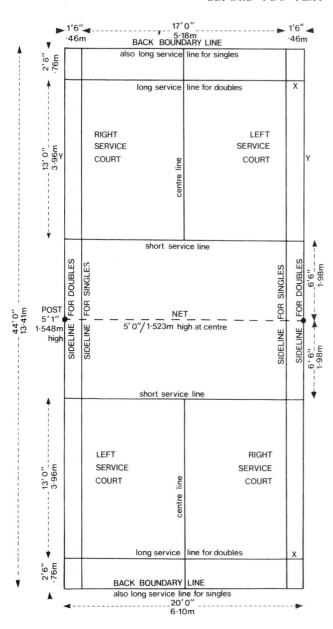

Figure 2 The official dimensions and markings of a badminton court. Note that the singles service court is longer than that for doubles.

the server's racket hits the shuttle. The shuttle must be struck from below waist level and the server's racket head must be below his hand.

He must not feint to serve or otherwise try to deceive the receiver except by the skill he uses in hitting the shuttle. If the shuttle is allowed to drop to the ground and falls outside the correct service court, the service is a fault and it is the receiver's turn to serve.

You have now read enough to go on a court and try to play a game.

Practice

Find a few old tennis balls and a large open space or tennis court. See how far you can throw each ball, making sure that you use the throwing action shown in *figure 1*.

Then buy or borrow some shuttles, go on a badminton court and from the short service line try to throw them over the net. If you find you cannot, move forward a little. The stronger your throw, the farther back you will be able to move.

Develop power through body, knee, arm and wrist action as described in this chapter.

Helper
Watch the thrower's arm action. Ensure that the throwing arm is parallel to the ground before the thrower's elbow bends to let the hand and forearm drop behind the back as far as possible.

See that the shoulders and left arm first point in the direction of the throw and then pivot to the facing position by the moment of release.

Watch to see that the thrower's knees first bend and then straighten with a snap to give extra power.

Ensure that the thrower starts with a relaxed wrist and arm so that both can flick forwards strongly at the moment of the throw.

2 Developing co-ordination

We hope you have now practised with a friend hitting a shuttle to and fro and have learned something about its flight; if so you should now be ready to start learning the correct racket grips.

The Grips

There are two basic grips from which all shots may be hit: the forehand and the backhand. It is important to understand the differences between them.

To obtain the forehand grip used by good players, take the racket in your left hand, holding it in front of you by the throat, parallel with the ground and with the strings perpendicular to the ground. Put the flat of your right hand against the strings, slide that hand down to the butt of the handle and then close the fingers as though you are shaking hands with the handle (see *figure 3*). Use your middle, ring and little finger to support the handle firmly, but not fiercely, and the first finger and thumb to hold the racket to obtain 'feel' and control the extent and direction of the racket's movement. Handle and swing your racket until it feels like an extension of your arm. The grip should be firm but gentle, rather than vice-like. This grip helps to free your wrist and arm from the tension which impairs muscle flexibility and destroys your sense of 'touch'. Only if your wrist and elbow are loose can you develop great racket-head speed, and make the variations of shot at different speeds, necessary in good class badminton.

Figure 3 The grips:
(a) Racket held level, hand flat on strings, fingers outstretched.
(b) The hitting hand slides down to the grip part of the handle.
(c) The fingers close to give the correct forehand grip.

Try this out for yourself by swinging the racket while gripping the handle as tightly as you can. Then use a less strained, looser wrist grip. The racket head can be moved far more quickly and in many more directions with the latter. The only time it is necessary to hold the racket tightly during and after a hit is when smashing the shuttle. This is primarily to stop the racket flying out of your hand. The foremost factor in successful stroking is letting the racket swing freely so it does the work. Once you start gripping fiercely and trying to force the pace, arm and wrist tension slows down racket speed and power is reduced.

Good timing means hitting the shuttle at the exact moment that the racket head reaches top speed. Maximum power is developed when the racket swing is along the line on which you wish the shuttle to travel.

Ensure the line is right by making your racket follow through along the line. Direction is governed by follow-through. Aim the follow-through correctly and your shoulders, racket, body and feet will automatically take up their correct positions along the line from where you are standing to your target.

Getting the grip absolutely right helps you obtain maximum racket-head speed. So use the hand-shake method and then check that everything is aligned by extending your right arm in front of you.

There should be a straight line running from the rim of the racket head, along the shaft, the handle, the 'V' formed by the thumb and first finger, the centre of the inside crease of the elbow up to the top of the armpit.

One slight danger lies in having the V slightly behind the handle instead of on top of it. Imagine you are about to knock a nail into a wall with the rim of the racket head; then the V can be checked. Precise positioning maximizes the effect of wrist flick and so adds power.

That found, spread the first finger a little from the others and let the thumb ride fractionally up the front part of the handle. This should give you 'feeling' between racket, first finger and thumb and so add sensitivity of touch.

To find the best backhand grip, take up the correct forehand position, arm extended. Bend your elbow so that your racket is across your body at chest level with the strings perpendicular to the ground.

Hold the racket firmly with your left hand and rotate your right hand towards your body until the thumb and the first finger V is in line with the two central main strings of the racket. Keeping the four fingers static, move your thumb upwards until it is along the handle and in line with those two central main strings. The V and all else should automatically fall into the correct position and your knuckles will be pointed towards the roof (see *figure 4*).

Figure 4 The backhand grip as seen by the helper. (*Above*) The correct grip. Note the position of the right side of the hitting hand (the fat of the hand). (*Below*) The wrong backhand grip with the back of the hitter's hand to the front. Use of this wrong grip minimizes wrist flick and so makes it difficult to clear consistently to the back tramlines.

Familiarize yourself with these grips. Then practise changing from one to the other until changing becomes automatic and needs no thought. Always check that your grip is absolutely right; inaccurate positions will not do (see *figure 4*).

The majority of the strokes are made with one or the other of these two grips. Gifted, natural highly competitive players, including most champions, do extemporize, though never out of laziness. When the situation demands something unusual, they instinctively come up with it, but only after a long apprenticeship. There are no short cuts to learning the correct grips.

The flight of a shuttle, with its high initial speed and ultra-low finish, obscures something which is very apparent in ball games involving a bat, stick and racket. It is that there are four kinds of beginners; 'pushers', 'swingers', 'throwers', and 'pullers'. Pushers include 'punchers'. There is an affinity between swingers and throwers. Pullers are the rarest breed. Badminton is concerned almost exclusively with swinging and throwing shots though one sees the occasional push near the net or a pull when the shuttle is returned desperately from low down and behind a player.

An imperative of stroke play for any ambitious player is full use of wrist flick, added to either the swing or throw of any shot. Most beginners automatically make some use of wrist. Experience and guidance normally develop this particular technique.

Refer back for a moment to the basic recommended grips and then test them for flexible range of wrist movement.

The Swings

Every stroke consists of three essential parts – back-swing, forward swing and follow-through. The most important part of the forward swing is concerned with the twelve inches (30 centimetres) or so before and after the point of impact of shuttle on racket. For simplicity and vivid identification this is usually referred to as the 'zip area'.

Backswing

The backswing prepares you for the stroke and should be made in the same direction as the fall of the shuttle. The wrist must be cocked – bent backwards – in all backswings, forehand and backhand.

In chapter one we emphasize that ninety per cent of badminton strokes are struck above shoulder height. For overhead strokes made on the forehand

Figure 5(a) Shows correct preparation for the overhead forehand shot with the racket dropping, the weight on the back foot, the head up and the free arm being used as a counterbalance.
(b) The racket has been thrown forwards and upwards towards the shuttle, the head is well up. The weight has already moved forward and the free arm is still being used for balance.
(c) The hit and follow-through have been completed. Weight is now fully forward, with only the hitter's back big toe retaining contact with the ground. Note how the right shoulder has been pivoted forcefully into the hit to develop greater power in the shot.

(the right side of a right-handed player) the back-swing demands the quickest possible upwards movement of the elbow and shoulder from wherever the racket finished the previous shot. The shoulder should be stretched up and back as far as it will comfortably go.

Your right elbow must be brought back and high enough for your right hand to be behind your head in the region of the back of your neck. Your wrist should be bent so that the lower part of the racket handle is touching the top of your shoulder. That is the best position for developing maximum racket-head speed, through the zip area of the stroke.

Forward swing

Turn again to the throwing pictures in chapter one to recall the correct action. Note how the hand at the moment of release is facing the direction in which the shuttle has been thrown.

Substitute in your mind a racket for the shuttle and visualize the throwing action. Pick up your racket and try it out – without letting go unless you have an old, broken racket and a lot of space. Then you can discover how far you can throw the actual racket!

The most effective means of achieving top racket-head speed is by striking rapidly and directly upwards at the shuttle. Avoid cramping the elbow. Ensure that it is always fully extended at the moment of impact. Both on the forehand and backhand you should feel a pulling in the right side of your rib cage as you stretch up to meet the shuttle and then hit it at the highest possible point.

Think of trying to open a cupboard that is out of your reach. The stretch feeling is identical.

Follow-through
The follow-through is extremely important. If you wish to develop maximum racket-head speed at impact there must be no attempt to slow racket-head speed until after the shuttle has left your racket strings. So think always of hitting through the shuttle; try to imagine you are hitting through to the front of it. It is similar to the way boxers are sometimes taught to think of punching their opponent's spine.

Hitting through the shuttle will also ensure that your follow-through stays on the line you hit the shuttle. This helps both direction and power. Let the follow-through flow unchecked; the arm itself is a sufficient brake.

The speed of the follow-through should vary in proportion to the power required.

Footwork

If badminton is mainly an overhead game, it is also a sideways game – the majority of strokes are begun with the shoulders facing one or the other sideline. Then, in time with the forward swing, the body should swivel from the hips, so that at the moment of impact the shoulders and hips both face the net; the position of the feet remains in the same area, but they also swivel to the front.

There is very little sprinting in badminton. Nearly all strokes entail either lunging, stretching, the chassé (skipping) sideways like a ballroom dancer, or stopping and starting. Your base of operations for singles should be central, just behind the front service line. Pace out the distances to the four corners of your court – they should all be the same.

Overhead strokes – clears, smashes and drops
In overhead strokes one is frequently forced backwards by a shuttle hit high over one's head so that it would land near to the back service line if allowed to fall to the ground. These 'clears', as they are called, are the equivalent of tennis lobs. So when your opponent clears deep, first take your playing shoulder back so that you are facing a sideline and then chassé until you are under the shuttle and able to point your left hand at it during its fall towards the ground. The actual hit is automatic if your first movement is backwards with your right foot in readiness for the chassé. Use your left arm to stretch your shoulder upwards, reach for the sky, watch the shuttle all the way down and throw the head of your racket up at it. Your eyes should remain on the point of impact for a moment after the actual stroke.

Take care to pivot your shoulders to the facing net position so that you obtain the full effect of body weight going into the hit. Let your body flow forwards with the hit. This should force your right leg to swing forwards and cause slight swivelling on the left foot.

The overhead clear is made when the shuttle has travelled too far behind your head to be hit downwards into your opponent's court. The power of the racket 'throw' is used to crash the shuttle upwards and deep into your opponent's court. This is the shot one normally teaches first.

If your backward chassé is rapid enough to take you behind the falling shuttle you can use the identical, full-power throw to smash the shuttle down into your opponent's half of the court.

The action is the same as the clear but the shuttle is struck in front of your head instead of behind it.

Midway between the points of impact for the smash and the clear lies the point of impact for the drop. The relative positions of body and falling shuttle are shown in *figure 6*.

Figure 6 The body movement of the overhead forehand is virtually the same whether clearing, drop shotting or smashing. The governing factor for which is used depends on the position of the falling shuttle relative to the hitter. If it is back as at A it should be hit vigorously towards the ceiling with the aim of clearing to the opponent's back tramlines. If the position is as B then a drop shot

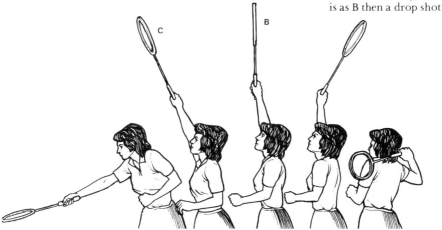

Recapitulating, overhead forehand strokes are made with the throwing action of a baseball pitcher, or a cricketer trying for a run out from a deep fielding position.

Underarm strokes

What about those ten per cent of strokes made when the shuttle has fallen near to the ground? That the shuttle is so low implies that you are on

is 'on'. If the player is behind the shuttle as in C then an all-out smash is probably the best shot. In A the body trunk will be inclined slightly backwards, in B upright and in C leaning forwards.

the defensive. So you are likely to be hurrying and possibly off balance.

This must not be taken as an excuse for sloppy stroke play. The more difficult the situation, the more you must drive yourself to move quickly in order to play the shot as perfectly as you can.

Most of the shots that you will have to return with an underarm stroke will be drops, usually near a sideline. Frequently you will be tempted to stretch with right foot forward when the drop is wide of your forehand.

Some people advocate this. Unequivocally, we do not. It is alarmingly difficult to hit consistently and accurately from the wrong foot – that is with the right foot forward for forehands. If your body is not in the correct position through wrong foot-work the stroke will be adversely affected. The swing is different and the hit is flatter. Power and accuracy both suffer. The shuttle can only be re-turned easily along the same line, in itself a disadvantage.

Those who teach the right hand, right foot system – and there is an alarming and worrying number of them – are concerned with recovering the shot and saving precious seconds. Just remember that if you go to meet the shuttle correctly and on balance, left foot forward for the forehand shot (and when you have worked hard and your footwork becomes instinctive you will virtually always have time) you will then have a complete range of shots from which to choose and will make them with a high degree of accuracy. You will be in command, be able to make a sensible choice of shot and therefore, will have time to recover. Be optimistic, be in control, do it correctly and arrive with all the choices still open to you.

Practice lunging because it is important for you to retain good balance. The more you can bend

your front knee and stretch your back ankle, the
longer will be your reach when lunging. Aim
at being able to reach all shots and then return
to base with just one long lunge. (Though children
may need a preliminary step.) If you cannot
manage this it is clear you are not lunging far
enough, so do something about it! Occasionally
your opponent's drop will place the shuttle out
of lunging reach. Do not accept this lightly. Make
a resolution that next time your lunge *will* take
you to the shuttle. Only an extraordinarily good
drop shot to either corner of the net will require
an adult to take a step before the lunge.

All shots should be learned correctly. You
should be striving to take every shuttle overhead.
When you cannot, do not try to hit it like a tennis
drive (a horizontal, forehand drive). Either bend
your knees so that you still keep the shuttle above
you or wait a shade longer for the shuttle to fall
lower, move into position, get your body round
and hit it as a proper underarm stroke. The
horizontal forehand drive at waist height is never
used in singles but used in all doubles, most
noticeably in mixed doubles.

The underarm forehand can be likened to an
underarm throw, but because time is usually
limited and you need to hit the shuttle as early
as possible, the backswing has to be short. To
compensate for this, the wrist flick and follow-
through have to be strong enough to do the work.
On the forehand side they will be sufficient as
you will be well forward and will only need
to hit the shuttle the equivalent of half a court's
length. As your game improves, you will hit more
off the backhand when defending. It is easier to
gain extra power from the use of your thumb, your
body is out of the way and the follow-through
leaves your racket in a good position for dealing

Figure 7(a) Lunging to
counter a short return
with a deep clear. Note
how having the left foot
forward positions the
body so that the racket is
lined up with the ap-
proaching shuttle, with
the hitting wrist cocked
backwards so that extra
speed can be imparted to
the racket head.
(b) The wrist has snapped
the racket head forward.
Note the head has re-
mained down, so
avoiding that jerking up-
wards of the body which
leads to so many mistakes.

with a rapid return. When the basics have been mastered variations and choices can be made, though any change in the stroke must take place only at the absolutely final fraction of a second before impact.

Returning drop shots
There are two basic replies to a drop, a return drop or a clear. As with overhead forehands, the underarm stroke has to be firm and flowing from start to finish. The swing must be stronger and firmer for clears than for drop shots. In determining which shot to use with a shuttle dropping close to the net you will find the following guide helpful. Picture the 180 degrees between your arm when it is hanging straight down and when it is extended directly above your head. For shuttles that have to be hit between zero and 90 degrees, assuming zero degrees is when your arm is hanging straight down, you should use an underarm forehand stroke. From 90 to 180 degrees think 'overhead', use the overhead backswing and lower or raise the shoulder to the required height.

For shots that are on the 90 degrees level, either bend your knees to use your overhead swing for an attacking shot or rise on tip toes to use an underarm defensive stroke. Conserve your energy at all costs and do not use a horizontal swing.

No matter how proficient you become with underarm or horizontal strokes, try to avoid ever having to use either. Aim to become so fast a mover and skilful an anticipator that you can hit every shot overhead. You won't succeed, of course. Your opponent's drops will sometimes force you to use the underarm forehand, either with a vigorous wrist action for clears or sensitivity for counter drops.

Nevertheless, seek with every scrap of mental and physical energy to raise your average of overhead shots from 90 to 95 per cent or more. Then, indeed, you will be a formidable player and one who derives great pleasure from playing.

Practice

1. Have a friend throw or, if he can play, hit a shuttle alternately to forehand and backhand, calling out which it is going to be and reminding you to change grip. Once you begin to show some proficiency start counting your shots to see how many you can make before missing. Do not try to rally with your helper unless he is a lot better than you. Instead, use four or five shuttles and have him throw or hit them one after another.

2. To practise throwing and using wrist flick take a shuttle in your playing hand. Stand in the 'T' junction on your side of the net. Throw to six different targets on the other side of the net (flat pieces of cardboard about a foot (30 centimetres) square will do). Make sure your follow-through is in a direct line to your target. You will have to put considerable effort into each throw.

3. To see whether you are loose enough with your grip to use your wrist vigorously, rotate your wrist with racket in hand so that its head makes a full circle. If you cannot make a full circle, keep on loosening your grip on the handle until you can. Later, this will be important for making delicate net shots.

4. To practice stretching and lunging forward for shots, have your helper throw shuttles gently over-head so that you can just reach them with one stride only. It is important for the shuttle to be thrown overhead as it simulates an actual hit which has passed over the net and is falling. Begin by standing in one tramline, with your helper in the one opposite, both of you on the same side of

the net. He should aim his throw at the line running down the centre of the court.

First, try only to reach the falling shuttle with one long lunge, then learn to use your wrist so that you can hit the shuttle back gently for him to catch.

Later move to opposite sides of the net and play late, low drops off your helper's throws.

Check points for helper

1. During practice routine 1 check to see whether the grip change is being made, by watching after the forehand and before the backhand to see that the 'fat' of the hand (right side) comes through first and that the back of the hand does not flop through (see *figure 4*).

The change to the forehand grip is usually automatic. Since you are not trying to sustain a rally, you can check that the change has been made correctly, before sending the next shuttle.

2. Check that the student's left shoulder, when carrying out the throwing exercise, is pointing towards the target area. Watch for transfer of weight from back to front foot, the swivel of hips and finishing follow-through.

For the deep throws it will be necessary at the end of the throw for the right leg to swing forward to maintain balance.

3. Watch the lunging to ensure that the correct footwork is being used. Make sure the front (left) knee bends really deeply. If the bend of the body is made incorrectly by the back, then the student's bottom will remain up in the air.

Net play practice

The lead-up to net play is to stand, or to walk

slowly round a court, hitting the shuttle up in the air with an underarm motion. See how many hits can be made when standing still. This is more difficult than when moving as more control is needed. Each time you play start with this exercise, first on the forehand and then, taking care to change the grip, on the backhand. Then alternate forehands and backhands. Record the score by means of a graph which each player should keep for himself.

The next step is for two beginners – or a beginner and any other player – on either side of the net to rally in the same way to each other, but giving the shuttle a slight forward hit at the same time. Practise wrist flick and hold the racket loosely.

To bring the shots down and make the hits lighter, use the area of the court in front of the service line only. Play a game with table tennis scoring (21 up) starting with a low serve from either X or Y in the diagram. All shots must be hit underarm and kept within the area.

This is an excellent exercise for beginners and experts alike.

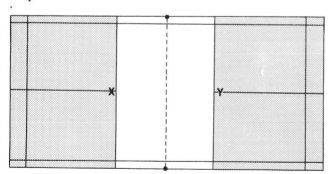

Figure 8 Developing net play. X and Y play a game of 'first to reach 21' using only the unshaded area of the court.

Helper
Ensure that student is changing grip correctly.
Watch that only one foot is in front of the short service line. The tendency is to creep nearer and nearer to the net.

3 The clear and the drop

The clear

The clear is basically a defensive shot. However, like the lob in tennis, occasionally it can have a semi-aggressive function when used, with expert judgement, as a surprise.

In its main role as a defensive shot, the clear will be made in one of four ways: overhead forehand, overhead backhand, underarm forehand and underarm backhand. Of these the overhead forehand predominates. Most clears should be hit high so that the shuttle descends perpendicularly as near as possible to the backline of the opponent's court. Clears are usually used in singles though they can be a valuable tactical weapon in doubles against a tiring opponent or one who is a little slow in moving from the front to the back of the court.

Both in doubles and singles a fast, low trajectory clear that just evades your opponent's racket, is a useful attacking shot, though it must be used sparingly.

The majority of your opponent's clears will be aimed at your deep, backhand corner. Many will follow a drop that has hurried you forward to a position close to the net.

So the first requirement is to be able to chassé (skip sideways) with great rapidity from any forward position to one that is underneath the shuttle when it falls towards your back boundary line. This must be combined with suppleness of body, especially of the back, so that you can chase back and then bend backwards to hit with your forehand overhead stroke, shuttles that are dropping on the backhand side of your body (see *figure 9*).

There is more to come. It is insufficient merely to make a good stroke. As soon as it is struck you should be hurrying back to your base in mid-court. The important thing to remember about court position is the paramount need to regain base urgently and immediately.

Supposing you are fractionally forward of base when your opponent clears to your deep, backhand corner. What then? Firstly, without letting your eyes leave the shuttle, chassé lightly and rapidly backwards in an attempt to place yourself slightly behind and in line with the falling shuttle. Your racket should be ready to hit. Watch the shuttle all the way to your racket strings.

Learn court geometry so thoroughly that you can tell with your eyes shut exactly where your opponent's back boundary line is from any part of your court. If you succeed you will be able to make an aggressive smash, a deceptive drop or, by adjusting position so that you can slam the shuttle upwards with a full-blooded 'throw' of your racket head, a clear. However, bearing in mind that the clear is essentially defensive, you will seldom if ever slam the shuttle upwards when you can smash it downwards at your opponent's half of the court.

When you chassé into position be sure to prepare your stroke early. Your backswing should be made with the quickest possible upward movement of your right elbow and shoulder from wherever your racket ended the previous shot.

Hitting the shuttle really high demands

Figure 9 The round-the-head stroke. The shuttle is falling into the backhand corner but the hitter has bent her back and is inclining her racket so that her forehand overhead can be used.

considerable power, so get your left shoulder well up and right shoulder down as far as it will comfortably go without upsetting your balance. Only then will you be able to hurl your full bodyweight into the upward hit.

Make good use of your left arm, not just as an aid to balance but also as a sighter for the falling shuttle by pointing it firmly and positively at that shuttle.

Bring your right elbow up and back so that your right hand is behind your head and you can, if you wish, touch the back of your neck. Your racket shaft should be resting lightly on top of your shoulder with your right hand almost in your right ear. Your wrist should be cocked, yet relaxed, in order to whip the racket head forward in the zip area.

This back swing should be made while you are moving into position and should be on the same line as the oncoming shuttle. Your body should pivot sideways to the net.

The forward swing links to the backswing through an almost imperceptible pause. If the backswing has positioned the arm, elbow and racket correctly, the forward swing must also be correct. It should travel the line along which you clear the shuttle, with the follow-through 'chasing' the shuttle upwards and forwards along that line vigorously and without pause at impact. Forward swing and follow-through should merge in an unbroken, flowing, vigorous throw of your racket head at the shuttle once more.

Apart from throwing your shoulders into the hit, care should be taken to ensure that the elbow is fully extended at the moment of impact. It should never be cramped. Stretch right up to hit the shuttle at the highest possible point. The racket strings should be slanted upwards so that

Figure 10 A useful exercise for teaching correct positioning is to draw a funny face on paper and then fix it to the student's left upper arm. Then feed the student with clears. If he turns correctly you will be able to see the face as on the player on the right. Beginners often prepare shots incorrectly as the player on the left.

the shuttle will rise off them at first. How far the rise and distance will continue depends on the strength of your hit, i.e. up and then on.

A part of your concentration will be concerned with regaining your central base and in this, the shot most frequently hit by all beginners and intermediates, the importance of early stroke preparation and position cannot be overemphasized. The two things go together. One should never by choice be moving backwards at the hit, though, inevitably, this does happen.

Coping with this situation demands flexibility of body and vigorous leg action in order to throw oneself forwards and upwards into the stroke. When preparation is correct the weight and body position is identical for a drop or smash, the transfer of weight forward being all important in obtaining a decent height and depth of clear. An arm alone cannot achieve it.

Underarm clears are usually made from near to the net, often when your opponent's drop is so short and low over the net that he will be able to crash down into your court any attempt you make to reply with another drop.

In going for drops lunge with your left foot forwards and at the shuttle. Your racket backswing should simulate an underarm throw but with the right wrist cocked upwards. It should be in line with the falling shuttle. The forward swing is first downwards and then rapidly upwards. The wrist snaps the racket head viciously forwards in the zip area and then combines with the arm in an unbroken swing until the elbow is forced to bend.

Still unchecked and flowing, your racket head should finally swing across your body towards your left shoulder.

Just before hitting the shuttle your hips should swivel so that your shoulders have turned from sideways to square to the net when you hit the shuttle. The feet should not move. Only after impact should your left leg push back from its forward lunge position to your base behind the front service line.

The hip swivel and wrist snap should be so timed that the racket head reaches its fastest speed at the moment of impact. It needs a lot of power to hit an underarm clear to the back line so you should seek to develop every factor which adds power to the racket swing.

Hit right through the shuttle and chase the shuttle with your follow-through. This must be a deliberate action. The location of the arm in relation to the body makes it simple to hit wrongly across the flight of the shuttle rather than along

Figure 11 The underarm clear at full stretch necessitates strong wrist flick. This is completed at the end of the zip area. The racket continues forwards and upwards vigorously with the eyes following the shuttle but no upwards jerk of the head and body. Meanwhile, see how the left leg is pushing strongly to help the hitter regain base rapidly.

the line of your hit. Hitting across the shuttle leads to loss of power and reduces accuracy.

The act of lunging forwards tends to drive the right arm backwards to counterbalance weight, so you must remember to prepare your stroke while moving.

For the forehand stroke your lunge should be made with the left foot forward. Important as this is, it is even more important to lunge with your right foot forward when reaching towards the backhand. This turns your body so that it faces the backhand sideline and you should accentuate this by pivoting so that your racket wraps around the left side of your body and you have your back half-turned to the shuttle.

From this 'wrap around' backswing, which must be made in the same direction as the fall of the shuttle, uncoil your arm in a forward swing. Pivot your body into the hit in harmony with this arm swing and snap your wrist into the hit.

The 'wrap around' backswing, cocking of the wrist and pivoting of your body can, when synchronized, develop tremendous power. The follow-through is related to the backward and forward swing and must flow on without pause. It is not something on its own but an integral part of the whole shot. Its flow should be in pursuit of the shuttle as it leaves the strings.

Lining up the backswing with the falling shuttle automatically ensures that your lunge lowers your body. Learn through practice to bend the front knee deeply, so as to keep your chest close to it. If you are stiff the bend will come from your hips, thus increasing the eye-to-racket distance and the likelihood of swinging at an angle to the shuttle instead of backwards and forwards along its coming and going line.

This makes good timing more difficult and increases the chances of erring, either in length or direction or both.

The drop

Continuous clearing or, if it were possible, non-stop smashing would surely prove self-destructive at any level of badminton between two players of equal standing. Variety is essential and in overhead play that variety is supplied by the drop shot.

Though there are variations of this shot at higher levels of the game, they all derive from the basic shot so it is essential that this be mastered.

Fundamentally, the swing of the shot is that of the smash. It breaks down into preparation, swing back, hit and follow-through. As soon as you see the shuttle cleared by your opponent chassé into position for a smash, if you can.

Take your racket up and back behind your left shoulder, taking care to line up with the path on which the shuttle is travelling towards you. Watch it carefully while keeping part of your mind on your opponent's position and the shots you have previously made in the rally.

Move quickly enough to be positioned for a smash but if you judge the moment is right for a drop, lean slightly forward so that when your racket contacts the shuttle it is in line with your nose.

Start your forward swing as if smashing but slow it down rapidly so that your hit is just strong enough to send the shuttle gently over the net so that, if allowed to drop, it will land only a foot or so from the net.

Though you slow your swing, continue your follow-through along the line you drop the shuttle. The drop may be softly hit but it is still a firm, positive stroke demanding a follow-through which flows rhythmically from the earlier part of the swing. It may be safe but it is an attacking shot.

The slowing down of your swing through the zip area will automatically shorten the follow-through but this must still be part of the whole stroke. Because the drop is a gentle stroke there is a tendency to believe that correct footwork, positioning, swing and the like are less important. This could not be farther from the truth. Indeed, tiny variations can make the difference between a good and bad shot, so correct technique is, if possible, even more important.

Practice for the clear

Because the clear is the shot most frequently used by players when warming up, it is automatically practised. However, this is not quite identical with rally play and so the exercise shown in *figure 12* should be used: it needs a partner who serves well. You (Y) start at the dotted circle. Partner (P) can have six shuttles ready for serving at quick, regular intervals to produce a simulated rally. After skipping back to 'H', Y clears into the target area. The total 'goodness' of Y's clears can then be measured by scoring where the shuttles fall. See how near to 90 points you can achieve.

Scoring can be carried out by P or, better still, a third person who can also add points or extract penalties according to whether or not Y returns to base after each clear.

Figure 12

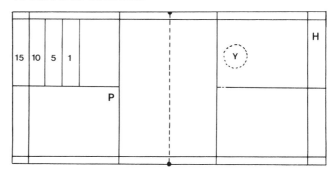

Practice for the drop

Whenever possible, practice routines should involve both you (Y) and your partner (P). In the exercise shown in *figure 13*, P sends over a high singles service deep to the forehand corner.

Y plays an overhead drop to anywhere along the net and returns immediately to his base in centre court. Y must have returned to base before P replies with another net shot to anywhere along the net. The rally ends.

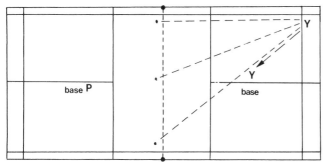

Figure 13

No matter how poor any of these shots may be, each player is able to use them to make the next shot. It is vital for Y to return quickly to centre court every time so that this eventually becomes automatic.

Guide to helper

See that P moves rapidly to base after serving and that he waits alertly, knees bent, weight forward, racket held up in readiness for immediate movement when he sees Y's return shot. Switch your eyes quickly to Y. See that his footwork (skip steps, please) is correct and that he returns to base right after making his drop shot. His follow-through must be soft and gentle; make sure that on the follow-through his racket head moves gently downward ahead of his hand (*figure 14*).

Look back at P to ensure that he returns the shuttle the moment it crosses the net, not later. Once he is able to hit the shuttle consistently he should stretch to it with a lunge, one foot only in front of the front service line. This area can be called the 'service sea'. One foot in it and you are safe, two feet in it and you drown.

Beginners find even this simple rally difficult and some or all shots in each rally may be poor. Encourage them to persevere; success eventually follows this simple start. To add stimulus, count each missed shot as one, the first conceding ten errors losing the game.

Figure 14 The Dropshot. Correct wrist finish by the nearer player, wrong finish by the far player. The racket head should lead the wrist.

4 Service

In badminton you can only score whilst serving. If for no other reason, that makes your service just about the most important stroke in the game. It is also one that can be practised alone so there is very little excuse for being content with a weak service.

Two types of service predominate, the high and the low. They are supplemented by a low-flying drive service, but this is seldom used by a beginner.

In singles, high serves are used almost without exception. However, surprise is the essence of shrewd tactics and one must never fall into the trap of complete predictability.

Dealing first with the high service then, the main object is to force your opponent right back into that extra two feet six inches (or 75 centimetres) of service court you have in singles compared with doubles. Hit high enough, the shuttle will fall slowly and almost perpendicularly, so giving ample positioning time and the maximum chance of reading your opponent's intentions. A shuttle falling perpendicularly is also most difficult for your opponent to time correctly.

In execution the high service is identical with the underarm forehand stroke except that you drop the shuttle into position with your free hand and you have not been hurried into a poorly balanced state by an opponent's well-placed shot.

Figure 15 The high service.
(a) Weight is on the back foot ready to rock forwards; the racket is held high at the back ready to begin the swing.
(b) Just after impact; the racket and hand are in front of the body, strings upwards and travelling onwards, weight is already transferred to the front foot.
(c) Follow-through, up and on, the right shoulder is well up, the back foot is balancing only on the toes as the full transfer of weight is completed.

The difficulty lies in dropping the shuttle into the ideal hitting position.

Start by positioning yourself about two to three feet (between 60 centimetres and one metre) behind the front service line and near to the centre line. Place your feet at a forty-five degree angle to the centre line, left foot forward, so that your body is neither square to the net nor facing the sideline. Ensure that your weight is on your back foot in readiness to rock forward as you hit. Keep a part of each foot in contact with the ground.

Now extend your left hand holding the shuttle by your thumb and forefinger just below the 'skirt' (feathers). Transfer your weight onto the front foot, then drop the shuttle and notice where it lands, about two feet (60 centimetres) ahead of your front foot.

Drop the shuttle over and over again, each time moving away from your service position so that you have to set yourself up afresh, just as you have to in match play.

Next, holding the shuttle in preparation for dropping, make a backswing with your racket, following gently and slowly with a forward swing until your racket and arm are near the imaginary perpendicular line down which the shuttle would have dropped had you let it go.

At this imaginary point of impact between racket and shuttle your racket face should be inclined slightly upwards. Because the shuttle falls about two feet ahead of your left foot (providing you began with the correct stance) the whole of your racket should be in front of your body.

If the racket face is perpendicular the shuttle will have travelled parallel to the ground and so under the net. If it is inclined too far the shuttle would have gone high in the air, possibly without crossing the net.

Half-way between these two racket-face angles is the one which sends the shuttle high, to that essential length in the 'tram lines' at the back of your opponent's court.

Having 'shadowed' the movement slowly, try hitting the shuttle. Synchronize the forward movement of your left arm, which will drop the shuttle, with the backswing of your right arm and racket.

Begin your forward swing as you release the shuttle. You may, at first, feel hurried, and so tend to rush at the shuttle. There is more time than you think. With a little concentrated practice you will acquire the timing that enables you to make contact at the desired spot in the swing of your racket.

For a strong high serve it is advisable to start with the right arm outstretched behind, hand at shoulder level and wrist cocked. This gives you a uniform start each time and allows a rhythmic swing and interaction of racket arm and body to develop. Far too many players start with shuttle and racket touching in front and then they sweep back the racket before swinging forward. This introduces far too many variables. The sweep-back varies, the wrist is forgotten altogether or the extent to which it is cocked changes from service to service, the actual line of the swing-back is not constant, and so on. So start with racket back and ready. Then the shuttle only has to be dropped.

Cock your wrist during the backswing, which should be along the line you intend the shuttle to travel. Snap the wrist in the direction of your hit during the moment of impact. Without check, keep the racket travelling fast and far along the line of your service until your follow-through ends with your racket over your left shoulder. Limitations of elbow movement will hamper you if you follow through towards your right shoulder.

Strive to make your swing smooth, rhythmic and continuous. The follow-through must be vigorous if you are to force the shuttle high and deep into your opponent's back court.

Remember, if you hit the shuttle very high it falls perpendicularly. This often provides a valuable guide to distance in many sports halls. Instead of vaguely trying to find the back service line with a number of practice serves, examine the court on which you will be playing before the game begins. Go to each end and look upwards for a distinctive rafter, line or lights or other guide directly above the doubles service line. Sight them again from your serving positions at each end of the court. Then, when serving, forget about the back line. Instead, aim at the target you have located, making that the high spot of your hit. The shuttle, because of its perpendicular fall, will drop time after time right in the vital back court area.

This system cannot be used in a low hall, where it is necessary to use the back lines as guides. This is one of the reasons why it is difficult to serve to a consistent depth in a low hall.

Equally, it is extremely difficult to serve in a vast hall like the Empire Pool, Wembley. There the roof is so high it can scarcely be seen. Furthermore, because of its size, there is always a considerable breeze which blows the shuttle off course and length.

However, all sports halls – as opposed to arenas – have a spot at which you can aim if you look carefully enough beforehand and imagine the downward fall of the shuttle.

A high, deep serve is absolutely essential for all singles until county junior or division one, adult league, standards are reached. When your opponent is strong enough to clear end to end, the other variations may be tried in order to keep him guessing. However, the high deep serve remains the main service right the way up to world champion standard.

Matches are won and lost on service. It is the one shot that can be practised alone but, sadly, one finds little evidence of this happening. You can only be satisfied when you can send eleven out of every twelve high serves unerringly into the back tramline. Even that achievement is no excuse to quit practising your service every time you go on court.

The high serve is not as suitable for doubles games. Instead, the low, short serve takes its place.

This should land, as first choice, on the junction of the centre and front service lines, the alternative being the wide, short serve which, ideally, lands on the junction of the front service and outside service lines.

So you have to learn four angles, two from the right court, two more from the left. Study the court until you can point precisely to each of these four points with your eyes closed. Indeed, you might try shadow serving with your eyes shut, opening them to check that your follow-through ends with your racket pointing exactly at your target.

It is absolutely essential when learning the low serve to memorize the height of the net so that it can be completely disregarded when actually making the service swing. Because the margins separating a good and bad serve are so slight, the stroke demands the utmost concentration. Clearing your mind of unnecessary thought about net height leaves you free to 'feel' strength and direction.

Take a perceptive look at the court to which you are serving and at the tape of the net. Then concentrate your eyes on the shuttle and fix them there until the hit has actually been made.

Figure 16 The low serve. *(a)* Preparation. *(b)* Point of impact, well below the legal height. *(c)* Gentle follow-through (compare with figure 15).

The racket for a low serve must follow through gently but firmly along the same line as the shuttle. It must travel forward rather than upwards since it is essential for the shuttle to skim low over the net; alert opponents nip forward quickly to kill shuttles which go too high.

When using the low service it is vital to keep the trajectory of the shuttle as flat as possible. This entails hitting it at a higher point relative to the ground than for a high serve. Lofting the shuttle over the net from the lower impact point (of a high serve) gives the receiver more time to rush forward to the net and also presents more of the base of the shuttle than with a flatter trajectory.

Obtaining that flatter trajectory by raising the point of impact increases the danger of faulting through making racket–shuttle contact above the waist. Rising on tip toe at the moment of hitting gives added inches but faults, actual and alleged, through raising the racket, lead to many tense moments in league play.

After making a low serve even beginners should take one step forwards to the 'T'. This helps to form the vital doubles formation position but it is one which all beginners find excessively difficult to take up. This is primarily because they cannot consistently serve net-skimmers and they are scared of the on-coming smashes which inevitably follow serves that send the shuttle too high over the net. Taking that step inwards when practising helps to develop the vital follow-through towards the net which keeps the shuttle low and safe.

Be alert. Expect the receiver to rush forward and punch the shuttle straight at you and so have your racket in position to parry the shuttle. If you are truly alert and the shuttle is not aimed at you, you will frequently find time to lunge and make surprising 'gets'. As your confidence and technique improve, so your returns of smashes will become less defensive and more varied. But always take that vital step forward from the moment you first learn the low service. It is immeasurably better to start in the way you intend to continue.

There are two recognized variations of the low basic serve, the fast, upward-rising flick and the fast, flat drive to the centre line. The drive is an advanced variation.

The fast, upward-rising flick is used in doubles as a surprise and to inhibit the receiver from always anticipating a low serve which he can rush. It is usually hit to the outward corners formed by the side and back service lines. Preferably produced with exactly the same preparation as for a low serve, the wrist is snapped through suddenly with increased speed and power just before impact.

New players should stick to the low and fast, upward rising flick as a variation when playing doubles. There is nothing to be gained by using a high serve because the back service line for doubles is two feet six inches (75 centimetres) further forward than in singles and so is not far enough back to prevent aggressive smashes by the receiver. Accept from the start that there is no alternative to learning and developing a sound, low serve, no matter how much effort and time it takes.

The fast, flat drive to the centre line can be a devastating variation but the target area is small and difficult to find so the element of risk is high. It is an advanced variation suitable only for players with considerable technical skill. Yet once acquired, this serve opens up all four corners of each service court, so increasing the receiver's uncertainty.

The corner which is chosen is often determined by the score in the game, one's nerve at the time, or by the apparent readiness and position of the receiver.

The low backhand serve is an extremely easy one to master but, as with all alternatives to the ideal, it has its limitations. If you choose to master this as your basic low serve you must accept that the limitations exist. You cannot drive serve, you cannot serve high and deep, you cannot easily serve short and wide to the right court, you cannot recover as quickly for the return shot to the net and you cannot vary your serving position on court from the central T junction.

With all these demerits the serve is nevertheless used at the top levels of play, county, international

Figure 17 The backhand serve.

and world standard, mainly because of its one big asset – being hit with the white shuttle held in front of white clothes and with the very acute threat of a flick as its alternative, it cannot be 'seen' until a moment after it has been struck and therefore it is almost impossible to rush. Add to this its ease of direction from centre line to centre line, the shortest distance possible, and you have a chance to play a perfect, if invariable, low service which is safe from attack (see *figure 17*).

The shuttle is addressed with a backhand grip while standing almost square to the net, right foot leading slightly to give the racket head room between body and shuttle. Body weight is on the front foot, head well down and over the shuttle. The strings of the racket are put against the shuttle at just below waist (and legal) level, handle, and thus hand, perpendicular above it. The eyes then rise to sight the net tape once more, and go back to the shuttle. Take a small backswing towards the body and then lightly stroke the shuttle forwards, following through forwards and then upwards to tape height. The racket must be held very loosely and the shuttle stroked gently without a jerk – or it will pop up and present itself to be 'killed'.

Many beginners who are not accustomed to racket sports find the low service action the most difficult to conquer. This backhand service is a good alternative which at least allows a player to start a rally safely and not become a total albatross to his partner. But do remember it is full of limitations.

Another alternative to the low serve, with many of the same limitations, is the pendulum serve. It looks cramped and ugly but has been used with success by all standards of players, up to world calibre. The action is again recommended for players who have no feeling of shuttle on racket after six to eight months of trying the normal low serve; those whose serve is still jerky, high over the net and consistently an immediate loser.

For this action lead with the left foot and put your full weight on to this foot. Hold the shuttle above your left toes, lean well over the shuttle and raise your right elbow as far back as you can behind you, to shoulder height (see *figure 18*).

The grip for this serve is quite different. The entire front panel of the handle of the racket faces forward. The hand moves around to the back of the handle with a loose grip of thumb and first

Figure 18 The pendulum
serve.

finger supported by the other three fingers. The
face of the racket head should be open (looking at
the net) and the strings parallel to the net.

Cock the wrist as far back as possible and then
drop the shuttle and allow a pendulum action to
take place from your racket hand, the racket
moving towards the shuttle gently but smoothly,
following through as far as the wrist will allow.

For both this and the backhand serve your extra
body-lean over the shuttle and the downward

angle of your head (as opposed to just a lowering of the eyes for a normal forehand serve) means that the opponent is at the time of starting the serve completely out of your view. Although a disadvantage to most of us, this actually helps those players who need to resort to this type of serve (as opposed to those who simply choose to serve this way) because a very tall or menacing opponent who might unnerve them still further is now totally out of sight, and possibly out of mind.

So, to end this chapter, perfect your high serve for singles, your low serve for doubles, continue to practise them even if you become a champion, and only when you are proficient with these two serves should you work seriously on the variations.

Figure 19

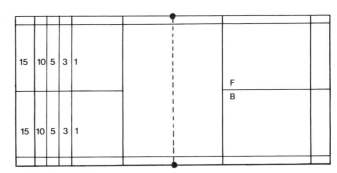

Practice

Mark the court with chalk as shown in *figure 19*. Send over ten high serves from F and note your score. Repeat from B.

Mark court with chalk as shown in *figure 20*.

Go to the other end of the court. From LF serve ten times to the target FS; then to FM, noting score each time. Move to LB and serve ten each to BS and BM. See *figure 20*. Repeat all as necessary. Progress is easily measured by day to day, week to week scores.

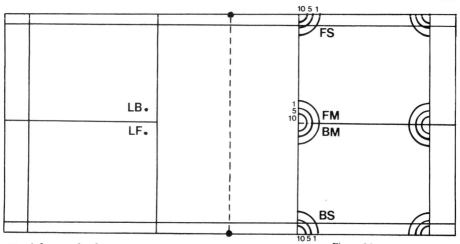

Figure 20

Guide to helper

On high serves, make sure the height is sufficient to pass above an opponent with arm and racket outstretched. Stand there yourself as a check and record each score when the shuttle falls; it can so easily move after landing.

Watch the server's swing, which should follow an identical groove time after time once a natural and comfortable swing has been found. Check that the follow-through flows from the hit and that the racket stays on line until the elbow 'breaks' to let the racket finish over the left shoulder.

On low serves see that the impact point of racket and shuttle is higher than for high serves. Watch that the backswing is shortened and the wrist cocked. Check that the follow-through pushes the racket head forward rather than upwards before the final upwards finish.

Note the height the shuttle crosses the net and decide mentally if you could have rushed forward and smashed it. If so tell the server to take a preliminary look at the net band, memorize its height, and then concentrate on the shuttle.

5 Backhand strokes

To repeat, badminton is a game in which ninety per cent of shots are hit above shoulder height. It is also primarily a forehand game, in which each player should become sufficiently nimble of foot and flexible of body and arm to hit with his forehand all but those clears which go deep to the backhand corner after he has been pulled short and wide to the forehand side line. And, even then, his aim should be to chase rapidly back to base from the forehand so that he can still skip quickly backwards in time to deal with deep clears to the backhand with a round-the-head stroke, be it a counter clear, smash or deceptive shot. If the shuttle cannot be hit on the forehand, it is probably better to let it fall lower and hit a backhand from nearer the ground, usually as a deep clear. This should be done with a long, deep lunge with shoulders, head, and nose deep down towards the ground. The eyes must be focussed on the falling shuttle. Clearing upwards from so close to the ground means that your racket travels more or less horizontally to the ground at first, curving into an upward direction as the racket enters into the zip area of the stroke. In such cases the right foot is usually well over towards the sideline in a long lunge which helps rapid recovery to base.

So a line between your feet will be roughly at right angles to the direction of your hit. Your shoulders should usually be in line with your feet, thus allowing your body to pivot clockwise to give added power. Your elbow and wrist should swing into the stroke ahead of your racket face, both snapping into the straight position during the zip area portion of your swing. Your thumb should be along the back flat of your racket handle, so helping to propel your racket into the hit along the line of your shot. This will help you maximize racket-shuttle contact time, so helping control and accuracy. It is as if your racket is trying to chase the shuttle.

Figure 21 Low backhand clear.
(a) Low backhand clear preparation. The wrist is fully cocked back, the racket head is wrapped around the body for full forward swing. Weight is held back.
(b) Just before impact. The arm and racket are unwrapping, the wrist is leading the racket head in preparation for snapping into the hit.

The remaining strokes are those made when your opponent forces you to hit the shuttle above head level on your backhand side. Normally it is struck as a clear but there are a few occasions when the return is short enough to permit a backhand kill. Both strokes are difficult for young players and novices and should not be taught to beginners, especially when they are young children. The swing demands strength and a refined sense of timing. Eventually these strokes must be added to one's repertoire, for no ambitious or advanced player can afford deficiencies of technique. Meanwhile, encourage the use of the 'round-the-head',

(c) Long, high, upwards follow-through. Weight is fully forward, the player is balanced only on the back foot.

Figure 22 The backhand clear made with an overhead stroke is inadvisable at club level because it is an advanced shot. Nevertheless, it is frequently attempted. So if you must (*a*), turn your back on the shuttle and let your weight fall on the back foot.
(*b*) Use your elbow to mark the line and fall of the shuttle.
(*c*) Hit the shuttle directly above the leading shoulder, transferring weight to the front foot.
(*d*) Let the arm and racket follow-through strongly along the line you hit the shuttle before sweeping downwards.

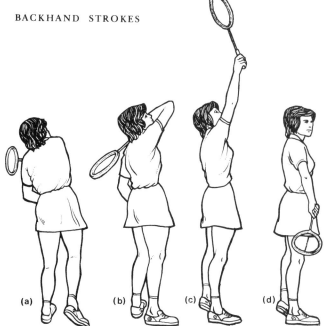

(a)   (b)   (c)   (d)

forehand smash or, if that is impossible because of the opponent's accurate placing, let the shuttle fall into position for the clear hit from around hip height (see *figure 9*).

But remember that ultimately you must become equally adept on both wings, no matter the height at which you make any particular stroke.

As with the forehand smash or clear, the backswing for these shots on the backhand should be along the same line as the fall of the shuttle. The backswing should be free and easy but if yours is restricted, then overcome this by bending both your wrist and elbow and by turning your body so that your right shoulder and, preferably, your right shoulder blade is turned towards the falling shuttle. This assists a free and easy backswing. Look over your right shoulder at the falling shuttle and glue your eyes to it all the way down to the point of impact.

To obtain the correct backswing pick up your racket with your backhand grip and reach for the sky. Your upper arm should be more or less touching your right ear. Cock your wrist to the left until your racket is parallel with the ground and the strings are facing skywards.

Move your arm forwards and then bend your elbow till your forearm is in line with your fore-head. Now touch the front of your chin with your upper arm and cock your wrist fully to the left.

Picture a fly in front of your head and close to the ceiling. Swat it fiercely with your racket face, snapping your wrist and elbow straight to develop extra power. Swat straight through that imaginary fly without checking your downswing; the back-swing, hit and follow-through should form an unbroken, flowing movement.

The backswing should line up with the falling shuttle and the follow-through should flow along the line on which you have hit the shuttle. This line should be duplicated by a line running from your shoulders to the heels of your feet.

In short, racket, shoulders, body and feet should all be in line with the direction of your racket swing. The backswing, with its use of elbow and wrist snap, can develop tremendous power but there is some danger of swinging the racket at an angle to the falling shuttle and the direction of your shot. This results in some loss of power and, more importantly, unnecessary and avoidable errors.

Recapitulating, high backhand shots demand precise timing and strength. They should not be used by beginners, novices and children but, in fact, most players will want to have a try. Use the 'round-the-head' forehand stroke or, if that is not possible, let the shuttle drop before clearing with a strong, upwards hit backhand.

Practice

To realize the potential power in the backhand
and to understand when this power is needed, try
the following:

1. Stand close to the net, right shoulder and right
hand and racket parallel to the tape of the net,
using a backhand grip. Cock your wrist fully and
with your left hand pull back the head of the
racket hard so that the pull of the left hand and
the push of the right thumb can be felt 'fighting'
against each other. Suddenly let go with the left
hand. The racket head should smack loudly and
crisply into the tape. This is the power in the zip
area, just waiting to be used. It is also the power
from just one wrist working all on its own.

See how far you can hit a shuttle with this wrist
movement. While you are near the net be hand
fed ten to twelve shuttles; tip the racket head
slightly backwards so that the shuttles will lift
over the net. Hold the head back and then zip
into the shuttle but, and this is important, don't
follow through with your arm. That's cheating.
Just let your wrist straighten and then stop. You
should be able to hit the shuttle three quarters
of the way down the court.

2. Now move half-way down the court and again
hold your racket head back with your spare hand
(this stops your taking a backswing and so cheating
again). Be hand fed shots which come to you at
knee level or lower. Because you are further back in
the court you will need more power to cover a
greater distance so you will need a follow-through.
A high follow-through after the action of the wrist
is completed, high racket, high arm, high shoulder,
and a forwards-lifting feeling in your body. You
should be able to hit to the same point three-
quarters of the way down the court area as before.

3. Now move to the back tramlines. Obviously you are a long, long way from the far end, nearly 40 feet (12 metres) and you will need *all* your power, body weight, pivot, backswing, shoulders and hips.

Wrap your playing arm thoroughly around your body so that the racket head is behind your back. Put your weight on your back (left) foot. Make a big, wide, heavy backswing when the shuttle is fed to you by racket anywhere from chest height downwards. Do not forget the zip area and the follow-through. You may find that your timing lets you down in the zip area.

Guide for helper

Backhand weakness, when the shots are totally lacking in power in comparison with the forehand, nearly always stems from the grip or the shoulder-blade. Of all badminton shot-faults, they are the easiest to see and to correct. If you are not feeding, then stand at the end of the court, behind the feeder. You are looking for the right shoulder-blade and the fat of the hand. If you are feeding you are perfectly positioned to see.

Another remedy is to get the player to lift his playing elbow up. This stops a tucked-in backhand emanating from the stomach. The elbow can usefully be used as a pointer, being aimed up and at the shuttle until the preparation is completed.

6 Dress and equipment

There are four primary reasons for taking care in choosing the clothes you wear for playing badminton. They are:

1 so that you can move and lunge easily
2 so that you look the part. This helps your confidence considerably and confidence is vital to success
3 so that you are completely protected against the cold or, in warmer weather, so that perspiration will be absorbed. This helps to protect you against unnecessary muscular aches and strains
4 it is stipulated in the Rules that you must wear white – except for the tracksuits worn for warming up.

Easy movement starts with athletic agility but is helped by the wise choice of the clothes you wear, both for competitive play and practice.

Most players use old clothes when practising but if shrinkage has made them too tight or repeated darning made them rough to the skin, they can easily lead to restrictions or inhibitions in your stroke play. These may affect the grooving process of your strokes or movements without your realizing it. And when you groove a wrong movement or shot it has to be ungrooved before the correct one can take over. Remember, championships titles are won on the practice court.

Worn shoes, short laces, tight socks with holes or darns, shrunken shirts or shorts – or voluminous ones – sweaters that have become board-stiff and too small through repeated washing, all these are liable to detract from your best performance in practice. Immaculate practice is one road to successful match results. So don't be penny wise and pound foolish. When in doubt, throw out.

Shoes

Your feet take a heavy pounding during a badminton session so a comfortable fit and adequate cushioning is tremendously important. There is little straight running but continuous lunging, stopping, recovering and turning, so a good grip is vital. Whether your shoes are light, medium or heavy in weight, is up to you but bear in mind that quickness is a function of your power-to-weight ratio so the lighter you and your clothes are, the quicker will be that vital first movement for each shot. Make sure all have reinforced toe caps because of the wear caused by dragging. Many types have heavy toecaps or special reinforcement up the big toe side. Good fit applies to socks also. Have as many pairs as you can afford and wash them repeatedly; after every match is best, though this is not always practical when you play several matches in one evening. Many players find it helpful to dust their feet with talcum powder before putting on their socks. This helps dry up perspiration and so diminishes the likelihood of Athlete's Foot.

Together your socks and shoes have to protect your feet from bruising and blister-producing friction; corns and bunions may be caused by an ill-fitting shoe. Think about all these things before going to a well-stocked shop to make your purchase. Be sure it has adequate equipment for

Figure 23 Badminton imposes special strains on particular parts of your shoes. This pair, by Relum, have deep rigid soles which extend backwards to cover the middle of the heels which are further strengthened by an overlay. The fronts are also reinforced by soft leather overlays over and along the big toe areas of each shoe; rather than over the whole of the front areas, as that might decrease flexibility. Foot flexibility is important in badminton.

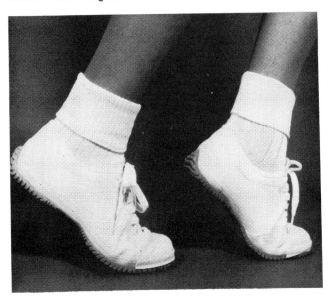

discovering your correct size and fitting. If you can afford it, we recommend that you buy two pairs of shoes at a time, once having established that the first pair are completely to your liking. They should be identical so that you can alternate them match by match.

In the case of socks, first make quite sure that they are pre-shrunk. All-wool socks tend to shrink more quickly than those knitted from man-made fibres, but the latter are non-absorbent. So we recommend socks made from a combination of both. The better quality chain stores usually stock a good variety.

Dress

We recommend a skirt or shorts and shirt combination, white in colour and sufficiently easy in fit to eliminate all restrictions of movement, always remembering that badminton entails lunging and stretching far more than running. For growing teenage girls, turn to those manufacturers who produce neat, all-round pleated skirts with Velcro expandable waistlines. Parents know only too well how boys grow out of clothes almost before they have time to wear them. Take care about the cut of shorts and, if possible, choose those with side adjustments that allow for growing.

Sweaters

You should choose a white sweater – apart from the rules forbidding colours, we think white looks better and we know that good appearance helps confidence. Ensure that your sweaters are loose but not floppy and remember that the object is staying warm before and after play or between matches. Badminton is played indoors so the

Figure 24 Suitable dress for badminton worn by M. Schnasse of West Germany.

thought of wind seldom occurs to players. But a few matches at the Empire Pool, Wembley – home of the All-England Championships – provide adequate proof that strong draughts, if not outright wind, can be found indoors, especially by the muscles of players who fail to protect themselves each time they finish a match. Make it a rule to put on your sweater immediately after finishing a match or practice session. Let the sweater be wind resistant and absorbent. And take a shower or bath and change into dry clothes at the first possible moment. Between matches in tournaments it may be wise to miss the shower or to limit it to a brief in and out for the sake of freshness and cleanliness but still change those clothes, especially all underclothes, including socks.

Underclothes and accessories

All underclothes, whether worn by boys or girls, men and women, should ideally be made from absorbent cotton. Over-knickers worn by girls should be neither too tight nor too loose fitting. They are always visible to people watching the play so thay should be considered as part of the general ensemble.

Long hair also may cause distraction, so be sure either to wear a towelling head band, hair grips or ribbons. However, you may discover, if you play badminton competitively, that shorter hair is more practical.

Rackets

This is your most important purchase so choose it carefully. Sound, powerful stroke play depends on good timing and the speed with which you can move the racket head. Since badminton rackets vary little in weight, before buying ensure that you can swing your prospective purchase freely.

Wrist flexibility is important so while making a few full-blooded swings flick your wrist during the imaginary moment of impact. Grip affects wrist action. It is a mistake for children to start playing with a cast-off adult racket. There is some danger of the grip being too large to permit or encourage the firm but gentle first finger and thumb grip that makes for maximum racket-head speed.

Even more important, the balance may not be right. Suitable balance is tremendously important. For young beginners a racket should balance on the middle finger at a point half way between the tip of the head and the end of the handle. Since the average racket is twenty-seven inches (69 centimetres) long, this point is thirteen and a half inches (34.5 centimetres) from either end of the racket. With such a balance there should be no feeling of heaviness. Bigger, stronger children and bigger adults may later prefer a racket with a heavier head but Judy Hashman has always used a centrally balanced racket.

Touch is experienced through finger and hand neural sensations and these are heightened by using a suitably sized and shaped handle grip. Too small a handle necessitates an over-tight clenching of the fingers, setting up tensions which are trans-mitted all the way up the forearm to the elbow. Shocks caused by mishitting or hitting the shuttle off centre can rupture small blood vessels, so causing tennis elbow. The effect is intensified when the fingers are tightly clenched around a handle that is too small. This clenching and consequent tension also inhibits the gentle yet firm use of the fingers essential for maximum wrist flick.

The handle can be covered with reversed leather, towelling or other suitable materials. Leather becomes greasy and needs roughing up with a wire brush. It is better when bound round the handle rough side out. This delays the time taken for it to become excessively greasy. Towelling is popular but it grows matted and hard very quickly. Apart from changes in feel, this ageing also brings about differences in handle size.

There are two types of racket strings, man-made and natural. Man-made fibres are considerably stronger and far cheaper than animal gut. Unfortunately, they are relatively lacking in elasticity even though manufacturers have made progress in improving this quality. Beginners and novices are unlikely to possess the sensitivity of touch common in good tournament competitors. This will change once they have reached the stage where they can forget about the details of technique; then their minds will be free to concentrate fully on how each shot feels to the fingers and hand. That, perhaps, is the moment at which to change from man-made strings to natural gut. Until then stick to the former unless you are so prosperous that the extra cost of natural gut doesn't matter.

Theoretically, the ideal shape of handle for reducing tension and maximizing 'touch' is circular but with a circular handle there is no way of telling, without looking, how the racket face relates to the shuttle. The best compromise, therefore, is a handle in which the front and side flats have a recognizable difference in feel. Yet over-riding all this is the need for individual comfort. So in choosing your racket bear in mind these factors. Remember especially the importance of supple wrist movements and their relationship to finger tension and buy the racket which, when you swing it in imaginary stroke play, feels like an extension of your arm and hand.

Nowadays steel-shafted rackets are all the rage. They are as flexible as wooden varieties but even though they are metal that is no reason for neglecting to keep them in presses and away from heat or dampness.

Racket headcovers are a 'must' as the game is played when all sorts of atrocious weather is going on outside.

Your racket should be tightly strung so that you hear a high pitched 'ping' rather than a deeper 'pong' when you flick the strings with a finger. Man-made strings being less resilient than gut, rackets strung with them should be marginally slacker to compensate for this.

If you are a beginner, try to play a game or two with a number of rackets borrowed from people around you, offering, of course, to pay for repairs or replacements if by mischance you cause damage. This should give you some idea of differences and help you to make a suitable purchase when the time comes to buy. Even so, seek expert advice when buying.

Once you graduate to match and then tournament badminton you will need two rackets in case one breaks during play. Look after both of them carefully, and prevent either one becoming your favourite by using each in turn. Any differences are far likelier to exist in your mind than in reality but psychological factors have a big bearing on results. No matter how poor your shot and bad your temper, always remember that it is you, not your racket that caused it. So never smack the floor or post or chair in rage; the only beneficiary from such behaviour is your opponent. At best he will be encouraged and at worst you will snap or bend the racket and so cause yourself unnecessary expense.

7 Improving your game

Once the basic strokes have been learned lose no time in refining and developing them. Champions are differentiated from lesser players mainly by qualities like ambition, determination, will to win, dedication, powers of concentration, a search for perfection and, yes, sheer love of the game. Compared with qualities of technique, these intangibles probably account for seventy per cent of the overall winning formula. But this in no way diminishes the need to develop technique, strokes, tactics and physical condition to the greatest extent.

If you go on court knowing you have practiced your strokes to the maximum, worked unceasingly to eradicate your weaknesses, studied your opponent, mentally rehearsed your match tactics, imagined all the eventualities that might arise and decided how to cope with them, trained assiduously and intelligently and ensured that your equipment and clothes are in top condition your mind should be free of all anxiety.

Do not confuse anxiety with nervousness. You should be nervous. This shows you are eager and prepared for the contest. Your adrenal gland is pumping away, physically sensitizing you for action.

If you have prepared to the limits of your current ability there can be no self-reproach if you lose. You have done your best. If that is not enough, analyze the reasons for your inferiority, get back on the practice court at the earliest opportunity and work on eliminating the cause of your inferiority. Maybe you will lose again when you next meet that same opponent, and the next time after that. But make absolutely sure that he does not win either of those matches for the same reason as he won the first.

The fool excuses or glosses over his mistakes. The wise man faces up to them and learns from them.

Nevertheless, never expect or accept defeat. Try your utmost for every shuttle that crosses the net, for each point that is played. Concentrate every scrap of your mind on judging the quality of each shot coming your way and treat it on its merits.

Even if your lungs are bursting, your heart pumping and your head throbbing from the exertion of a long rally or series of long rallies, never fall into the trap of trying to force an end to the rally, because the odds will be against your making a winning shot. Summon up your courage and will to hit one more good return, and one more, and one more, until your moment comes, then, and only then go for the kill. Realize that you are fighting a battle of your will-power against his, and be absolutely determined that yours will not be the one to yield. In order to maximize this effort it is essential for you to be free of anxiety. There should be no tiny 'if onlys' to disrupt your mind at seven-all in the final game. That is not the moment to regret a slight inability to lunge an extra six inches. That deficiency should have been rectified weeks, months or even years before.

Correct, thorough preparation not only develops technical skill but it adds to the mental tranquility which is so vital in championship matches. A couple of late-night parties with new, exciting friends are great fun, but your memories of them fade far more quickly than those of the championship you lost simply because you weren't quite sharp enough to 'read' the drop you could have killed at fourteen-twelve in the second game.

Having accepted the need for thorough preparation and intelligent practice, how does one set about it? Firstly, understand fully the object of practice. It is to ingrain so thoroughly a movement or series of movements, or sequence of shots, that they can be completed perfectly and completely automatically time after time, even under conditions of pressure and strain.

Movements are caused by electrical impulses transmitted to the muscles by the brain via your neural system. Each message 'burns' a microscopic passage which makes it minutely easier to repeat the message and movement next time. Thousands upon thousands of repetitions develop a so-called 'groove'. However the correct groove is only one of many that might be burned into the nervous system. Indeed it is just as easy to groove a wrong shot as the one you need to develop. And once grooved, a wrong shot will have to be erased and replaced by the correct one.

That is why it is so tremendously important to concentrate every bit as hard in practice as you would in match play, despite the fact that practice play does not provide the stimulus of an opponent to beat. In fact there is someone better present – yourself. You may not end the session with any clear-cut decision like fifteen–ten, fifteen–eleven. But if you are honest with yourself, you will know whether you have ended the session a fractionally better player than when you began it.

If you truly feel that you have achieved this, then you will have 'won' that practice session. That is important because World Championships are won on the practice court. So, when practising, concentrate completely on all things you are trying to do. In that way you will groove them so thoroughly that in match play you will be able to trust your body to repeat them automatically. This will free your mind to think about tactics, analyze your opponent and so on.

It is similar to driving a car. At first you have consciously to perform every action as well as to steer the car. When you become proficient the car more or less drives itself while you concentrate on the road, making slight corrections, as necessary, from time to time.

In learning situations you should not be put under pressure. Your mind needs freedom to concentrate on sending the right orders to your muscles. As proficiency advances so pressure may be applied, but never overlook the need for pressure-free practice to concentrate on correct grooving.

In learning, or developing your stroke play, change fairly frequently from stroke to stroke; a few minutes on the forehand, then on the backhand, then service, clearing and so on. Then back to forehand and through the other strokes again, but in a different order. The length of time that you should spend on one particular stroke depends on your powers of concentration.

When you have been through the full range a couple of times try to string all the strokes together in match-simulating sequences.

8 Concentration, anxiety and nervousness

Positive action is the most effective antidote to anxiety and wandering concentration. In badminton the best way of achieving this is by concentrating totally on the shuttle – in other words, treating each shuttle on its merits (TESOIM). This involves judgement which demands intense, discriminating, applied concentration. Ask yourself, 'Is it fast, slow, deep, short, straight, wide? Can I attack? Should I defend?' These and other questions concerning your opponent's position on court, his strengths, weaknesses, likes and dislikes and favourite shots, all have to be answered virtually at once. So TESOIM when applied with complete purpose should focus the mind fully on the rally being contested. There will be no time for concentration to wander, until the rally ends.

In dealing with each shuttle strictly on its merits and backing it with inflexible determination not to err, thoughts about winning or losing the match have no part in stroke-making. Each rally is a personal contest between you and him – your lungs may be bursting but you know that you are going to win it. Under such circumstances anxiety will be a million years away and the feeling of arousal and nervousness will give you the physical and mental energy to go on to the death.

But what happens at the end of the rally? Or series of rallies? Now, perhaps, comes the momentary distraction of noticing someone you know watching the game, or the worries about the close rival you will have to meet if you win.

It is useless to counter with thoughts such as 'I must concentrate'. You can be so busy concentrating that you forget completely to move forward for an unexpected short serve.

Instead, accentuate the positive. Project your attention forward to the next point. Assess the situation created by the rally which has just ended. If it has been long, strenuous and you have lost it – consider momentarily your opponent's state. Unless he, too, has read this book he may well be relaxing fractionally with the relief of winning that rally. It could well be that a sharp, unexpected return will find him reacting just that shade more slowly and so missing, or giving you a simple shot.

Alternatively, you may decide to wait for your opportunity and so let another long rally develop. Again, resolve that you won't be the one to give up. Be sustained by the thought in the back of your mind 'This may be killing me but I'm prepared for it. It's much worse for him'. So stay with him. Never surrender. TESOIM, until 'its merits' offer the chance of a kill or winning drop. Remain so mentally alert that you see that chance in a fraction of a second, and immediately find the physical energy to take that opportunity.

Playing with this mental attitude leaves no room for wandering concentration or anxiety. Such an attitude makes the game exciting, stimulating and pleasurable, and you will probably become so involved in it that there will be no room for 'vacuums' even between rallies.

Nevertheless, there is a limit to the length of

time over which even the greatest expert can avoid losing concentration. Furthermore, it is difficult for most people to sustain a long term, philosophical state without thinking forward to an outcome. But looking forwards is the arch enemy of the stroke-by-stroke concentration.

The answer is to substitute the long term prospect of victory, which may turn out to be the bitter one of defeat, with something shorter and more quickly realized. The process is called 'fragmentation' and it is simple to apply. Remembering TESOIM, try playing your matches two rallies at a time, vowing that you will win at least one of them. This will give you immediate targets and an immediacy of purpose that may well prove advantageous for most of your career.

Fragmentation possesses an advantage, additional to its value as an aid to concentration. If you concentrate on winning the rally when your opponent serves you often win the next rally also and so score a point yourself.

There is one further valuable aid to concentration, especially when your opponent's pressure is hurrying you into technical mistakes. It is to focus your mind on one particular facet of your strokes. Ensuring that your backswing is in line with the oncoming shuttle, is one thing to try. Possibly taking care to follow through along the line of the shuttle you have just struck, is better. Seeking to make each shot as soon as possible after the shuttle has crossed the net may be best of all, since that involves judgement of pace and length with consequent movement, and demands that you watch the shuttle from the very moment your opponent hits it. Before then is even better, because as you gain experience you will often be able to 'read' his shots before he actually makes them and so become skilled in anticipation.

So next time your attention starts to wander or you begin feeling anxious about the result or how you are playing, accentuate the positive with this three point plan:

Concentrate on one important technical point, e.g. taking the shuttle as soon as possible after it has crossed the net.
TESOIM.
Start fragmenting, and keep your eyes within the court.

Avoid 'hamming it up' because you mistakenly think it looks good. If you feel anger and excitement within yourself this will probably show in your face. Recently American research has discovered that if you are internally tranquil, but look irritable, your look will quickly 'feed back' and your tranquillity will give way to irritability.

Anger, irritability and anxiety all spoil good performances. So for your own sake, look, act and stay composed. You will be less than human if your hackles never rise. When they do, take two or three deep breaths, controlling both intake and output of air, move slowly into position and look calm. Not only will this help you but it will deprive your opponent of any lift he might derive from seeing you losing self-control. People will soon start telling you what a wonderfully calm player you are. The more you are told this, the more you will believe it and the calmer you will actually become.

Maybe your opponent will begin acting up. Never fall into the common trap of copying him. You are *you*, we hope a leader not a parrot-like mimic, so retain your individuality.

If you are nervous before a match, be thankful. It shows you are keyed up for action and that you are physiologically ready for the struggle. Make the nervousness work for you by flooding your mind with what you intend doing. Picture in your mind as vividly as possible the details of the match to come and imagine yourself winning.

You may experience flutterings in your tummy or perhaps slight breathlessness, leaden legs and an arm as stiff as steel. If so, sacrifice a point or two by hitting and moving with all the freedom you can muster. Or concentrate on something definite like watching the shuttle with exaggerated care or working at obtaining maximum wrist movement. Experience will teach you what helps you best. Having discovered it, practice it regularly, even when you are not tense. Then it will eventually become as automatic as an utterly exhausted Guardsman's response to a command.

Above all, enjoy the challenge and the game itself. Even if you find yourself one day in the final of the All-England Championship or representing your country in a Thomas or Uber Cup match, still remember badminton is a game to enjoy, that enjoyment makes you play better rather than worse and that playing better and trying harder is the key to bigger victories.

9 Fitness

Many people play badminton simply for recreation and fitness. Others are more ambitious, with minds focussed on club, county, national or even international honours. Either way, some attention to general and special fitness should yield more than adequate reward for effort. Apart from improved health, even the rawest of novices should gain in suppleness and rhythm. This helps stroke play. And let there be no doubt that there is greater satisfaction to be gained from a smoothly struck stroke, hit on the 'sweet spot' of the strings, than from a crude miss-hit off the frame.

Because this book is mainly concerned with novices and intermediate players we shall not outline any intensive, highly specialized routines for would-be champions.

Firstly, what are the factors which make for improvements? They are, in no special order, skill, speed, suppleness, strength and stamina. Our object in this chapter is to tell you how to develop suppleness, speed and stamina. The extent of your improvement in these areas will depend on your ambition and the way in which you apportion the time and energy you have available.

Taking stamina first, this derives from the heart, lungs and efficient use of muscles. A superbly engineered jet engine runs more smoothly and is capable of working longer and with less stress than a mass produced, internal combustion car engine. Similarly, a well engineered (trained) set of muscles puts out more effort for less energy expenditure than an unskilled set which is out of condition.

The lungs take in fuel (oxygen) from the air. This is conveyed to the muscles by the blood which is pumped around the circulatory system by the heart. A greater oxygen uptake and more powerful heart action combine to feed the muscles more lavishly. There is a simple way to improve both. The method is running, mile after mile of it. How much and how often depends on your goal and your self-motivated determination to achieve it. Irrespective of this, running is superb for general health.

The specifics – stopping, lunging, etc. – need detailed training for improved performance. They are all a function of power. Power is a combination of strength and speed. For any given degree of strength, speed is inversely proportional to weight; the heavier you are, the slower you will be at starting, stopping, etc.

If you are really keen to improve, seek to increase your power to weight ratio by increasing your strength and ridding yourself of every ounce of superfluous weight. This necessitates expert and individual analysis and guidance. A word of warning. Beware of dieting so severely that you actually lose strength and any desire to eat.

Twisting, turning and stretching impose strains on the legs, hips, back, waist, stomach and rib cage. If you are highly ambitious, we must emphasize the need for individually planned programmes. Those who are less ambitious should try tuck jumps; that is leaping on the spot, bringing your knees right up to your chest with each jump.

Potato races are also valuable. Scatter half

a dozen golf or table tennis balls around a small waste paper basket, none of them more than five yards ($4\frac{1}{2}$ metres) away from the basket.

Start from the basket, run to one of the 'potatoes', pick it up, return to the basket and put – not throw – it in. Without pausing or stopping, run to each of the other 'potatoes' in turn, returning to the basket each time, until all are safely in it. Drive yourself as hard as you can, use your playing hand and turn first one way, then the other when picking up and placing in the basket. Imagine as vividly as you can that you are contesting a rally with racket in hand.

Remember with these and all similar exercises that there is a limit to their transference value. The main improvement will lie in your ability to do tuck jumps or run potato races. So always imagine they are part of a badminton game. A strong mental picture of yourself playing badminton whilst exercising maximizes transference value.

Lunging exercises, perhaps when carrying light weights (10 to 20 lbs; or $4\frac{1}{2}$ to 9 kg) are important. Aim at maximum stretch and speed but do not overlook balance. Remember that increasing your ankle flexibility will increase the length of your lunges; your back foot can add or subtract six inches, depending on how much or little stretch and flexibility there is in its ankle.

In order to maximize your quickness in starting and stopping, ensure that your above-the-knees front and back leg muscles are well balanced in strength. The back muscles are important for quick starting, those in front for stopping immediately. Most modern gymnasiums have special equipment for developing this muscular balance. Short sprints, twenty yards (18 metres) or so up and down a steep hill, are also very effective, providing that each sprint is timed and that you are constantly striving to reduce your times.

Do not neglect side lunges and the development of strength and flexibility in your back. Badminton is essentially an overhead game in which your back works hard, much of the time through arching.

One simple exercise is to lie flat on your back, legs straight out. Then bend your knees up so that your heels are close to your thighs. Using only your shoulders, lift your body clear of the ground until it forms a bridge from your knees to your shoulders. .Hold the position for ten seconds, lower your body to the ground for one second, form a bridge once more for ten seconds and repeat ten times in all.

To reduce dangers of injury, always spend time warming up with light, stretching rhythmic movements before starting serious exercises and movements.

In training it is generally true that the longer the time taken in building up to a peak, the longer you are likely to stay there. A crash course initiated three days before a match is likely to do more harm than good. If you really are keen to win your club championship give yourself two months of preparatory training and purposeful, intelligent, varied practice.

Remember that no coach or helper can put in what God left out but there are usually more things within than one believes. So it is up to you to forget what you may or may not possess, believe that you are lacking nothing and strive to the limits of your time and strength to develop every facet of yourself. Seek the help of your coach or mentor in doing this.

No elixirs can make you fitter than you are at the moment of taking them. Only training can do that. What sensible eating and certain supplements *can* do is to keep you at your peak for longer periods of effort. Do not trust everything you hear about diet.

Take the old 'steak for stamina' theory first. Full digestion of meat protein takes something like six hours. Any still in your stomach when you start to exercise tends to remain there.

So take in your necessary quotas of protein and fat after your day's exercise and restrict yourself to energy-giving carbohydrates on match days. There are certain energy-giving supplements available which contain carbohydrate as glucose syrup, mineral salts to aid the replacement of those lost in sweat and a relatively low fluid volume to avoid gastric discomfort.

Many match points are won through a surprising change of pace, sudden attack, unbelievable 'get', etc. which would not have scored in the early part of a match against a fresh opponent and special supplements help to maintain stamina and concentration during a match.

Finally, sleep. Success at badminton, be it at club or championship standards, imposes considerable mental strains. Tranquillity helps to overcome them.Try to discover your best time for going to bed and for getting up. People vary enormously but badminton is an energetic game and, as a rough guide, teenagers and players in their early twenties should be thinking in terms of nine to ten hours, two of them preferably before midnight. A warm bath, a glass of chocolate or milk, a little meditation and a well-ventilated room help.

If sleep is elusive avoid panic. Let your body relax completely. Try to keep your thoughts pleasant and tranquil. Rest the body and the mind. Then the ill-effects of sleeplessness will be minimal, certainly far less than if you worry and fret wishing for sleep to come.

10 Practice routines

At the risk of being repetitive, we want to state that the most important part of badminton is practice. The unflinching self discipline of hitting thirty or forty consecutive smashes, then clears, followed by drops, each one with every scrap of effort concentrated on mechanical perfection, is paramount.

Such sequences are unlikely ever to occur in matches but practice should always be more demanding than competition, be it mentally, physically or both. Simply going on court with someone, warming up for five minutes and then playing three or four games is totally inadequate if maximum improvement is your object.

In the early years of playing badminton my sister, Sue Peard, and I (Judy) developed a variety of practice drills which covered most of our needs. Repeatedly I demanded of our father 'teach me a new shot'. Later, after marrying Dick Hashman and moving to Abingdon, I discovered the wonderful facilities available back in Baltimore were now things of the past.

I was now restricted to two or three, one hour sessions a week with Dick as my willing, enthusiastic and inventive practice partner. Every minute of each hour had to yield a hundred per cent and so we refined and developed the routines Sue and I had used so successfully.

Far from abating, my desire for perfection

increased and we added new routines to help the development of new strokes and tactics and the elimination or reduction of errors.

For fifty minutes we would pound through a series of disciplined drills, ending with an all-out game to string them all together in a scoring situation. Since we were both tired by those fifty minutes of intensive routines, we usually played that game in a state approximating to the third game of a championship match. Thus will power and determination were given a thorough outing.

The drills that follow do not exhaust my repertoire. Any lively, ambitious aspirant should add to those outlined with imaginative drills of his own. Imagination and inventiveness are vital to progress. Without those qualities you cannot advance beyond what has been done before and in merely copying you are unlikely to reach the same levels of skill as the originator. So when practising give full rein to your creativity and ability to extemporize.

Now for some simple drills in which you will be 'Y' and your partner 'P'. Both of you are assumed to be right-handed. It is unnecessary for you to be of equal standard. So long as you have both reached moderate club player levels, you are capable of carrying out the drills with internationals, to the benefit of both.

The explanations may seem long and involved. Do not let this deter you. Read them first, take this book to the court, try each drill in turn and you will find they are all simple to understand.

Practice Drills

1 A general loosener *(Diagram 25)*
You (Y) and your partner (P), stand in the centres of your own courts. Y hits a flat, sidearm cross-

Figure 25 Stay on position 1 until you are thoroughly loosened-up and warm and until you are hitting 30–50 shots without missing. Then take one stride sideways to position 2 and repeat. It is important to reverse

court shot to P's forehand. P hits the shuttle straight and flat to Y's backhand. Y hits flat and cross-court to P's backhand. P hits flat and straight to Y's forehand. That completes the sequence pattern. Without pausing, Y starts the sequence all over again by hitting the shuttle cross-court to P's forehand, P replies to Y's backhand and the pattern continues as before.

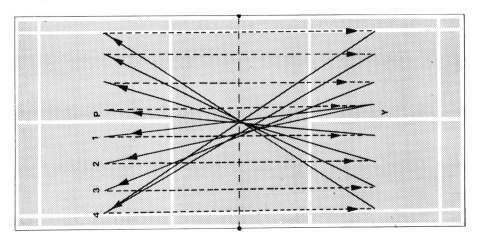

roles in each sequence so that both you and your partner have equal opportunities to hit straight (the harder shot) and cross-court (easier).

Count the completed rallies of four shots, the first forehand counting as 1 and each subsequent forehand of his 2, 3, 4, etc. When 10 is reached, switch roles and when 10 is repeated three or four times, move sideways to position 3, etc.

This pattern has you hitting cross-court shots and your partner replying with straight shots. Start the sequence slowly and hit the shuttle a foot or so over the net. Always use the correct racket grips and footwork. Gradually increase the tempo and widen and lower the trajectory of the shuttle until you have worked up to a fast pace. Lunge for each shuttle rather than sprint. You will have to move very quickly if this pattern is followed through correctly. Some sprinting will inevitably become necessary as the angles become wider but take care to end each sprint with a controlled lunge so that you can recover base correctly by pushing back with the forward foot.

Continue until you are both feeling warm and perhaps, are breathing hard – maybe even missing easy ones after previously maintaining fast, enjoyable rallies. When you start making stupid mistakes at this stage it is important to STOP.

2 Half-court shots *(Diagram 26)*

Y and P stand halfway down their own courts just within the sidelines and opposite one another. Y hits a low forehand half-court to P's backhand, lofting the shuttle well over the net and within the sidelines. P returns to Y's forehand who hits back to P's backhand, and so on.

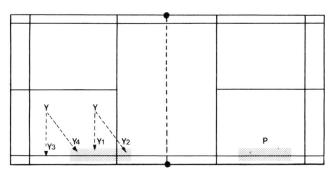

Figure 26 Y and P loosen up by standing correctly and hitting half court shots from the tramlines. When both are ready, Y1, Y2, Y3 and Y4 are the four places from which Y hits his shots, all of them to P's shaded area. The shuttle should be hit after one stride. Always concentrate on accuracy through correct footwork and balance. Y2 hits are made by Y moving in earlier, taking the shuttle higher and hitting flatter but still maintaining complete accuracy. Y3 and Y4 hits are made later (as if from a deep doubles or man's mixed position). They require more of a hit and a longer drive forwards on the stroke.

Please note that a half-court shot is solely a doubles shot and this must be uppermost in your mind when practising it.

After ten shots have been hit by each player and they have become familiar with the shot, both should start moving back to centre after each hit. This simulates the right-to-left and left-to-right chassé movements you would be making in match play. You are also likely to be forced into some deep stretches or last ditch lurches to reach some of those fast sinking, half-court returns.

Your thighs will tell you how effectively you are practising this drill. When they really begin to protest about the vigour of your movements, move nearer to your sideline until you recover a little. Then move back to your central base. After you and P have each hit fifty shots, stop.

Move over to the other sidelines and repeat the exercise, but in reverse roles, with Y hitting backhands and P forehands. Again, carry on until you and P have each hit fifty shots.

3 Smashing and a return drop

Using only one side of the court, Y hits a short clear to P who smashes at the inside sideline. Y returns with a straight drop. P sprints or lunges forward and hits a short clear to Y. Y smashes at the inner sideline, P answers with a drop, Y replies with a short clear, P smashes, and so on.

So Y and P are practising smashes and drops in turn. Go easy on the smashes at first, concentrating on accuracy, the downward angle of the shuttle and correct footwork. As the rally continues step up the power of the smashes, eventually seeking to bury the shuttle with each smash. But even at full power keep aiming for the sideline.

Keep the clears short and the return drop shots long enough to give the smasher a chance to keep the rally going.

As you become more adept at handling the smashes, try standing further back so that you will have to lunge for the smashes. Then move forward to try cutting off the smashes at waist height. But remember that returns made from the short position should, in this routine, be played to mid court otherwise the rally will end summarily.

After each player has hit ten smashes in the right-left court, move over to repeat the drill in the left-right court, but as it takes a fair degree of skill and considerable effort to complete a full, ten smash routine you may find it preferable to keep to one side of the court for an appreciable length of time before switching over. This allows time to become accustomed to, and so correct, some of the problems. Five minutes may be better than ten smashes before changing over.

4 The running round-the-head smash

Y starts in the right hand court with P opposite him. Y hits a loose drop shot to P's backhand who lofts a short cross-court clear to Y's backhand. Y runs across and hits a round-the-head smash down the line to P's forehand.

P replies with a straight drop and Y clears back-handed across the court to P's backhand. P moves over and hits a round-the-head smash to Y's forehand. Y hits a straight drop to P's backhand and so on.

When Y and P have each hit ten smashes, move over to the other sides of the court and begin from the left. Use the same sequence, beginning with a not-too-difficult drop. This time each player in turn will have to smash down the line when hurrying from left to right.

This is a somewhat neglected shot which some players cannot manage at all and a great number only very inaccurately. They tend to hit wide, either because they are late in moving under the shuttle or too hurried in execution to remember the exaggerated follow-through necessary for full power and accuracy.

Because this is a more beneficial, disciplined exercise than (3), continue with it until each player has hit thirty smashes.

5 Dropshots *(Diagram 27)*

Y stands deep in the right hand corner of his court, P opposite him at the net. P hits twenty-five high, deep clears to Y who replies with twenty-five

Figure 27 Dropshot, practice in countering. P has the choice of three positions for each sequence of 50 shots. In *(a)* he is positioned near to the net practising hitting the shuttle just as it crosses the net and lifting it to a uniform height and depth, taking care that his footwork is correct. Y hits 25 straight drops and 25 cross court.

(b) P moves to P2, lunges in for each drop shot and then recovers to P2 before lunging forward to P1 *(figure 27(a))* again.

(c) P moves to and from P1 for each drop shot from P3, a position he might find himself in after a deep, punishing clear which did not allow him time to recover to central base. This is the most difficult drill for achieving a uniform, straight feed from position P1. For varied drops, straight and cross-court, P keeps one foot in the service sea. Y has to cover his large, shaded area. P allows Y time and Y tries to outplay P.

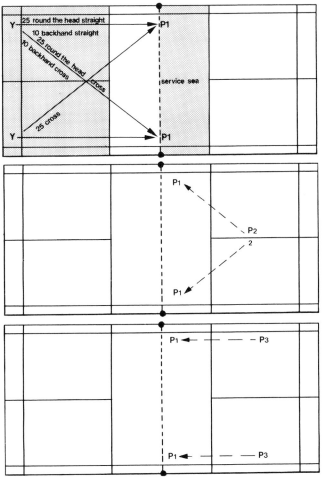

straight dropshots to P. P should hit the clears as identically as possible.

After twenty-five, P moves to the other end of the net, hits another twenty-five high, deep clears which Y tries to drop cross-court.

Next Y moves to the deep backhand corner, P continues with clears, and Y tries twenty-five round-the-head and straight dropshots followed by ten straight, high backhand dropshots. P then moves back to where he began and Y hits another twenty-five round-the-head cross-court dropshots, plus ten high, backhand cross-court dropshots. Then the roles can be reversed for P to practise drop shots.

The feeder need not be completely subservient in this exercise. He can and should move back to the centre of the court after each of his clears and then sprint in for the expected drop.

He should practice hitting the shuttle first at its earliest after crossing the net and then at its latest, simulating a last ditch lunge in so doing. In varying his methods but still concentrating on producing strings of identical clears, he can improve his control while developing his mobility. This is also a good form of on-court stamina training.

After each player has completed his quota of one hundred and twenty dropshots it is a good exercise for P to vary the length, height and direction of his clears and Y the direction of his drop shots, and vice versa when they switch roles.

If Y tries to outmanoeuvre P around the net in order to win a point and P moves the shuttle about so that it is only just within Y's reach, some deeply testing rallies can be experienced. At this first stage the feeder, P, should have the option of hitting half-court and flat shots in order to bring Y under total pressure. Y can then be pushed to wait at the back of the court, brought in to play underhand shots near to the front service line or have to intercept flat passing shots. The main task of P is to keep the shuttle within the possible reach of Y while Y must strive to out-manoeuvre P.

6 Clears

Start from the right hand court with Y hitting a high, deep serve to P who replies with a clear to Y's backhand. Y clears backhanded down the line to P who replies down the line with a clear to Y's backhand. And so on until Y has hit five backhand clears and P five forehand clears.

To switch roles P serves from the right court to Y's forehand, and so on. This is a somewhat tedious and severely testing drill, especially on the stomach muscles. It only becomes practicable after Y and P have played enough badminton to have gained some proficiency with the high backhand clear. This is not a drill for novices.

7 Associated half-courts

Y and P try to manoeuvre one another around using the front halves of their courts.

The object is to develop deception and accuracy when making and returning half-court shots in any direction. In order to ensure maximum exercise and leg movement the two players should strive to outplay one another, without hitting any shots downwards. Playing the best of ten points, scoring regardless of who is serving, and changing service, table tennis fashion, after every five points, introduce a modicum of competition which may increase effort.

8 Pattern rally play

Y hits a high singles serve from the right hand court. P clears to Y's backhand corner. Y hits a round-the-head drop to P's backhand corner of the net. P replies with a straight drop shot and Y picks it up by the net with a cross-court clear to P's forehand. P clears deep to Y's backhand. Y plays a round-the-head drop to P's backhand corner of the net. Continue as before. This may be varied by using the same rally sequence using the left (second) court for the service.

(b) Y hits a low singles serve from the right

hand court and P replies with a straight drop.

Y clears deep to P's forehand corner. P plays a clear cross-court to Y's forehand. Y hits a cross-court drop to P's forehand.

This is the equivalent of the opening moves after serving and the sequence is repeated.

This sequence taxes P severely because of the awkward, straight back chassé movement followed by the punishing cross-court clear which he then must hit. So Y must adjust his drop to give P time to recover.

(c) Similar sequences, with P serving. Then first Y and then P serving in the left court.

Both players should try to keep the rallies going. They should not end with Y or P scoring with a placement but only when one or the other misses his shot because of sheer fatigue. You will soon discover that an overhead clear at the end of a long rally is the most tiring shot of all.

Each rally should be accomplished ten times and six different patterns should be efficiently and energetically carried out in a practice session. This entails around forty shots each in every pattern. Allow a few moments between each change of pattern to mentally rehearse the next.

Having worked through your quota of six different patterns, you will have used nearly all the shots in the singles game. You should then realize how short the majority of rallies really are and have a greater appreciation of the importance of accuracy, consistency and applied concentration.

The patterns provide enough variety to stop your falling into a state of waking sleep and they make the session disciplined and purposeful.

Finally, string everything together with one normal game in which both of you draw on every scrap of physical and mental energy in trying to win.

11 Tactics

The essence of good tactics is surprise, at least at moderate levels of the game. Because a badminton court is relatively small, surprise must be allied to skill and accuracy in finding all four corners of the opponent's half of that court from every square foot of your half. That is why it is essential to practise clears and drops to every part of the backcourt and along every part of the net.

Simultaneously, alertness of mind, foot and body must be developed so that you can spot and pounce upon the very first loose shot played by your opponent in each rally. At the beginning the main difficulty is in spotting it.

When serving your primary aim should be to force your opponent right to his back line, first by the length and height of your service, and subsequently through the consistent depth of your clears. Your object is to produce a return which is weak enough for you to end the rally at once with an unreturnable smash or to set him scrambling with a drop.

This involves ability with three shots, the clear, drop and smash. In your early days aim safely inside the lines, with your drops well over the net, in order to avoid ending rallies with unnecessary mistakes.

In the beginning you and your partner should concentrate on achieving positive improvement with each session you play; improvement, rather than winning should be the aim.

Strive quickly to make the basic grips, stances, shots and ideas completely automatic. That will free your mind to concentrate on winning the point and the ways of doing so. This may reveal deficiencies in your stroke and tactical repertoire so you will need to devote a further period of time to learning. Then back to winning tactics and so on.

When attacking, then, probe the farthest corners of your opponent's court. Try to manoeuvre him so that he leaves gaps for your winning smashes or drops.

Maybe a fast, low clear will score after you have hurried him forward through a deep clear followed by a drop. Or a wrong footing, fast return to the spot from which he has just sped might be a point winner. His court is only seventeen feet (5.1 metres) wide but it is twenty-two feet (6.6 metres) long. That offers more scope for change of length than for exploitation of width.

Be patient in moving your opponent around the court. Maybe you have developed a splendid four-stroke pattern that frequently produces the shot for you to kill. However, your opponent fails to oblige with that gift. Too bad. There is only one thing to do. Start your pattern all over again and strive for the simple return that didn't happen last time.

But at the same time be careful to avoid stereotyped patterns which you repeat continuously so that your opponent knows in advance what will happen next.

When you are forced to defend make frequent use of a deep clear to the middle to his back line. And regain your base at once. Depth to the middle of his back line reduces the angles open to him for winning placements, kills or drops.

Never try the impossible just because you feel the rally has lasted too long. Stick with him, determined that you won't be the one to break down and even though you may be gasping for breath, will yourself to pounce on any loose shot he may play.

Doubles

You may be at the very peak of your form but unless your partner is also holding up his corner of a doubles, you will lose. Maybe not so decisively as when you, too, are below form but what does that matter when you are watching an official write in your opponents' names instead of yours on the draw sheet?

The lesson should be obvious, work with your partner. Strive to set up positions in which he can leap in for the kill. If he is doing the manoeuvring, position yourself well 'off the shuttle'. It is all too easy to look alert yet be locked in position watching his shots and so miss the chance of nipping in to end the rally.

In doubles the name of the game is attack. Lose an aggressive outlook and you are as good as beaten.

There are two basic formations which are known by the positions taken up by the server and his partner. One is called the front-and-back, the other the side-by-side. Once the shuttle has been served there is no discernible difference between these two formations; the game becomes a combination of the two.

In the less popular, more defensive, side-by-side formation the server and his partner both begin half way down the court, each in readiness to cover his own rectangular half of his pair's court.

Using the front-and-back formation at the start,

the server stands as close as possible to the T junction with his partner three or four feet (2.7 to 3.6 metres) behind him and slightly to one side or the other so as not to be unsighted. From his position he can see the preparation and delivery of the service and so gain some inkling of the possible return by the receiver.

The server conforms to the general rules of attack and defence by moving forward behind low serves. He is then positioned to cover the front third of the court from sideline to sideline while his partner covers the back two thirds.

Because he can see the serve being produced, the partner can quickly move to the side-by-side position as soon as the server delivers a drive or high serve. Because he is not unsighted by the server the partner suffers less chance of being caught by a half-court push behind his partner.

When the serve and its return are over, the serving formations become one. The key to success lies in attack, which, in doubles, means hitting the shuttle downwards whenever possible, be it with a full-blooded smash, a soft 'half' smash or a drop shot.

When attacking one player will be hitting the aggressive, downwards shots from the back two-thirds of the court while his alert partner should be keyed up to pounce on any loose return from his position at the net, with a deft drop or swift downward hit.

It may seem that the back-court player is doing all the work but he is hitting aggressive shots which should be forcing defensive returns so he has ample time to cover this greater area of court.

Meanwhile, by darting around the net with his racket up in readiness for a decisive interception, the forward partner is imposing severe psycho-logical pressure on the defenders; they know that a weak return will mean loss of the rally. So they are likely to continue with clears until one is short enough to be killed outright.

It doesn't always work out quite like that. The opponents may be too strong or fast, you and your partner too slow or lacking in the power or sensitivity of touch to finish the rally when the chance arises. So a surprising return may suddenly rob you of the initiative.

When this happens you and your partner will be forced to clear. No matter which one of you actually hits the shuttle, both of you must immediately move into the side-by-side formation in order to cover your respective halves of the court.

Remaining in a front-and-back formation virtually makes your opponents a gift of the rally. Sheer geometry makes it impossible for the back player to cover two thirds of a court against smashes which leave the opponents' rackets at great speed, and that sheer pace gives a front player little or no chance of getting his racket on the shuttle except by luck or seeming clairvoyance that 'reads' the smash before it is actually struck.

When forced on to the defensive you play ninety per cent of your shots under the pressure of pace or placement. There is scarcely time to think and you hit the shuttle almost by instinct. This is your moment of test. No matter how harassed and hurried you may be, you must still strive to think while hastening to return the shuttle. As a beginner you may find this impossible, but try nevertheless. As you move into the novice and intermediate classes keep on striving to think clearly. As your stroke play develops and becomes more automatic you will find more of your mind free to realize what is happening and to try consciously to change the pattern of the rally.

Appendix A: Scoring

There are three units for scoring, namely points, games and matches.

There is no set rule about how many points make a game. In men's singles and doubles it can be the first to reach either fifteen or twenty-one, depending on what has been arranged beforehand. In women's singles the first to score eleven wins the game; in all forms of doubles it is fifteen.

All sanctioned senior tournaments use the best of three games to decide the winner of each match, with an eleven points game for women's singles and a fifteen points game for all other events, except in cases when 'setting' is necessary (see below).

Some school events use one game of twenty-one points to find each winner. All round-robin (American; all play all) tournaments use one game of twenty-one points.

The contestants change ends on completion of the first game and, if a third and deciding game is needed, again at the end of the second game. In any third game ends are changed when the leading player reaches eight in a fifteen points game, six in an eleven points game, and eleven in a twenty one points game.

Setting

There are seeming, but not actual, complications

when the score in a fifteen points game reaches thirteen all. The player or pair who first reached thirteen then has the option of 'setting' the game to five. In this case the score is called 'love (nothing) all' and whoever scores five points wins the game.

The option may not be taken up. Then if the next two points are shared and the score becomes fourteen all, the player or pair who first reached fourteen has the option of 'setting' the game to three. The score is called 'love all' and whoever scores three points first wins the game.

In ladies' singles the first to reach eleven wins the game. If the score reaches nine all, whoever reached nine first can 'set' the game to three. If the option is not taken up and the score reaches ten all, whoever reached ten first has the option of setting the game to two.

Appendix B:
Beat the 'Pro' game

This is a game which is excellent for all standards and particularly for beginners as it encourages consistency. It also engages a lot of children on one court.

The spare children stand in line along the left tram line (see *figure 28*). A becomes the pro, B challenges him and serves. If A wins the point he scores 1 and B goes to the back of the queue. C then challenges A and serves.

If A wins the point his score goes to 2 and C goes to the back of the queue.

If C wins the point he takes A's place as the pro and A goes to the back of the queue. C does not score a point. Only the pro can score.

Then D challenges the pro and serves. If C wins the rally he scores a point. If he loses the

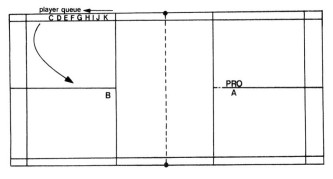

Figure 28 Beat the 'Pro' game.

point he goes to the back of the queue and D becomes the pro and is now able to score.

E comes on court, serves, and the game continues.

The challenger always serves, only the pro can score; the pro is always on the same side of the court.

The game can continue for a given period of time, say twenty minutes. The player with the highest score is the winner. The points won by a player each time he is pro are added together; he does not lose his points when he ceases to be pro and returns to the queue. Usually everyone ends up with at least one point.